Contemporary
Canadian
Architecture

For our parents

EDWIN BERNSTEIN
PHYLLIS BERNSTEIN

EDGAR CAWKER
MARJORIE CAWKER

with love and gratitude

Contemporary Canadian Architecture
The Mainstream and Beyond

Ruth Cawker & William Bernstein

Fitzhenry & Whiteside

Cover design: Darrell McCalla
Front cover photograph: The Mississauga City Hall,
                        Mississauga, Ontario
                        Jones & Kirkland
                        Architects, 1987
Photo Steven Evans

Back cover photograph: The Seagram Museum,
                       Waterloo, Ontario
                       Barton Myers Associates,
                       1983
Photo Timothy Hursley/The Arkansas Office

Fitzhenry & Whiteside Ltd.
195 Allstate Parkway
Markham, Ontario, Canada L3R 4T8

Canadian Cataloguing in Publication Data

Cawker, Ruth, 1953-
  Contemporary Canadian architecture

Rev. and exp. ed.
Authors' names in reverse order on first ed.
Bibliography: p.
Includes index.
ISBN 0-88902-733-1

1. Architecture, Modern - 20th century - Canada.
I. Bernstein, William, 1954-   . II. Title.
NA745.B47 1988   720'.971   C86-095050-6

We would like to thank the Ontario Arts Council
and the Canada Council for their kind assistance in
the production of this book.

Printed in Canada

Contents

Preface

The post-war era has been an intense period for the construction industry and for the development of architectural attitudes across Canada. With the ever-increasing accessibility of international architectural publications, Canadian architects are continuing to re-evaluate the direction in which they have been moving and toward which they are heading in the future. Several recent developments — the imminent opening of the Canadian Centre for Architecture, the choice of architect Melvin Charney to represent Canada at the 1986 Venice Biennale, expansion of the Canada Council's Architecture Division to award promising young architects a "Prix de Rome," and the awarding of major commissions such as the Paris Opera and the Phoenix City Hall to Canadian design teams — attest to the participation of Canadian architects in the larger design community.

What will hopefully emerge from this increase in theoretical activity surrounding architecture in Canada is a clearer sense of national and regional traditions of building and urban design. Research into pre-war writings by architects like Percy Nobbs and John Lyle has already begun to unearth the roots of a distinctly Canadian architecture, one that is attuned to local culture and climate. At the same time, studies in specific fields of Canadian art and culture provide a necessary counterpart to this historical awareness.

This book attempts to take part in the growing debates about modern architecture in Canada. Concentrating on major public commissions, we have chosen projects that are accessible to the general public. A thorough discussion of other areas, particularly housing, would require another volume. We have viewed the most significant directions of the years following the Expo '67 World Exposition in light of the historical and cultural contexts in which architecture has evolved. The book is organized in six interrelated sections to address these important contextual concerns.

In the first chapter, Expo '67 is discussed as a manifestation of the heights to which liberalism ascended in the late 1960's. The architectural implications of individualism, egalitarianism, and internationalism are reviewed within the context of the fair and Canada's centennial year.

The second chapter of this revised edition looks at the aesthetic attitudes of the country's most established architects, and how these have been shaped by a powerful clientele, in this case the National Gallery in Ottawa. The "mainstream," identified as architecture that is prescribed to a large extent by its clients' concerns and expertise, is viewed in light of various competitions for the Gallery, on the occasion of the building's public opening in 1988.

In contrast to Expo '67, and to architecture as an embodiment of liberalism, the third chapter examines the relationship between the conservation movement and conservative cultural attitudes. Major urban conservation projects in Halifax, Montreal, Ottawa, Toronto and Vancouver are discussed in depth.

The fourth chapter looks at the impact of conservationist tendencies on large new-construction projects. Government-initiated guidelines, together with the popular appeal of rehabilitation and infill, have effected discernable changes in the urban environment. Public space is the focus for examining the nature of these changes, which have often been accompanied by a heightened appreciation of social and cultural traditions.

The fifth section discusses the possibility of a reconciliation between the freedom of forms, materials and spaces inherent in modern architecture, and the constructive attitudes towards the environment provoked by conservation.

A new sixth chapter explores the tendency of innovative architects across the country to question the efficient ensemble-making that typified both mainstream and reform architecture in the post-war period. While this questioning may be the outcome of different regional or stylistic factors, it nevertheless centres on a common interest in the language of Canadian architecture, a vocabulary of images that is proving as varied as it is full of vitality.

Acknowledgments

The authors are indebted to William Dendy and Penina Coopersmith for their help in preparing the 1982 edition of this book. By generously making available his own research into historical subjects in Canadian architecture, Bill Dendy played a key role in the original shape of the book and subsequently reviewed a preliminary version of the manuscript for this revised and updated paperback edition.

We would also like to acknowledge the assistance of the Canada Council and the Ontario Arts Council; grants from both agencies made possible much of the travel and research for the preparation of the book.

In the course of our travels we were assisted and encouraged by many people.

In Victoria, we would like to thank Dan Savard.

In Vancouver, we were assisted by Michael Ames, Gerry Brewer, Robert Collier, Arthur Davies, Barry Downs, Arthur Erickson, Rainer Fassler, Andrew Gruft, Richard Henriquez, Bill McLennan, and John and Patricia Patkau.

In Edmonton, Brian Allsopp, Douglas Cardinal, the Cawker family, Barry Johns, Richard Schick and Joseph Shoctor were of great assistance.

In Ponoka, thanks to Ed Clarke.

In Calgary, we express much gratitude to Martha and Randall Chappel, Harold Hanen, Michael McMordie and Jack Long.

In Winnipeg, we would like to thank J.M. Badertscher, Harold and Donna Cawker, Lionel Ditz, Etienne Gaboury, Ron Keenberg, J.G. Pincock, Gustavo da Roza, Michael Rattray and Peter Tittenberger.

In Toronto, we express our gratitude to George Baird, Marc Baraness, the late Hans Blumenfeld, Charles Cansfield, Howard Cohen, Paul Cravit, Jack Diamond, Ronald Dick, Dan Dunlop, Oscar Duskes, Robert Fitzhenry, Susan Ford, Adele Freedman, Robert Hill, Robert Hopewell, Jan Hughes, Edward Jones, Helen Katz, Michael Kirkland, Eileen Mak, Pamela Manson-Smith, Joe Medjuk, the Department of Fine Arts at the Metropolitan Library, C. Blake Millar, Raymond Moriyama, Barton Myers, John C. Parkin, Hugh Robertson, Frederick Rounthwaite, Barry Sampson, Helen Sinclair, Lorne Tepperman, Donald Schmidt, Tim Shortreed, Peter Silcox, Heather Strongitharm, G.S. Vickers, Ted Wickson, Arthur Wood, Eb Zeidler, and Boris Zerafa.

In Ottawa, gratitude is due to Jean Boggs, Arthur Capling, Guy Desbarats, Mirjana Lakich, Claude Lavoie, Gyde Sheperd, Deborah Tunis and Dr. H'sio Yen-Shih.

In Montreal, we were assisted by Ray Affleck, André Blouin, Melvin Charney, Gary Dvorkin, Luc Laporte, Céline Larivière, Peter Rose, Victor Prus, Jacques Reeves, and Moshe Safdie.

In Halifax, thanks to Allen Duffus, Elizabeth Guilford and Tony Jackson.

In New York, our thanks go out to Edwin and Phyllis Bernstein, the late James Bernstein, Donald Clinton, Robbie Jamieson, Nancy Hahn, Jean Roberge, Erica Stoller, Nigel Thompson and Karen Wilkin.

I *Terre des Hommes*

To the more than fifty million people who came to visit it, Expo '67 presented an unforgettable picture of Canada at a particular stage in its growth as a nation. In keeping with the country's internationalist, peace keeping self-image in the 1960's, Canada's unique history and culture were downplayed. Instead, the emphasis was on a kind of perfect, state-less individual and a world wherein such individuals were equal. There was little room for the equally important collective and hierarchical values of Canadian society. All this was made abundantly clear through the environmental medium of the fair, the temporary city that was Expo '67.

One of the earliest decisions made in planning the fair was the choice of "Terre des Hommes" as its theme. The title of one of Antoine de Saint Exupéry's books, *Terre des Hommes*, told the story of France's first generation of commercial aviators, and the dangers and risks associated with their trade. Roughly translated into English as "Man and His World," it was up to a meeting of intellectuals to make of the book a theme for a world's fair.

A "theme-meeting" was held in Montebello, Quebec in 1963, attended by architects, lawyers, artists, authors and, strangely enough, a neurosurgeon. Responding to the theme of heroic individualism underlying Saint-Exupéry's depiction of the first generation of commercial aviators, the conference proposed that the fair celebrate the place and potential of the individual in a world of progress and change. In this regard, Saint-Exupéry was quoted: "To be a man is to feel that one's own stone contributes to building the edifice of the world."

To this emphasis on the individual was added its corollary in liberal thought: equality among individuals. Author Gabrielle Roy, one of the participants at the conference, summed up the group's "one firm basis of accord" as "faith in progress," but further explained the concept of progress in egalitarian terms, as opposed to the more usual scientific ones. "Progress," explained Roy, "should signify an increasingly equitable human distribution of misfortune and advantage. To progress then would mean to work towards a gradual '*rapprochement*' of all men of every condition and origin."

Saint-Exupéry, however, did not depict *all* men as heroic individuals; in *Terre des Hommes* aviators are, but bureaucrats are not. In choosing to quote Saint-Exupéry, the conferees had to do so quite carefully and selectively. For example, Saint-Exupéry had written of freedom that it "leads to equality, and equality leads to equilibrium, which is death." "If there is no hierarchy," he wrote elsewhere, "there is no brotherhood."

Most significant in the theme for the fair which emerged from the conference was its purposeful omission of nationalistic sentiment. Despite the fact that it was Canada's hundredth birthday, Expo '67 was not to explicitly promote or celebrate *Canada* (or any other nation for that matter); the theme of the fair was to be, at once, the individual and the world at large, with very little in-between. "The entire development," concluded the conference, "shall reflect the primacy given to human values and apirations in the theme '*Terre des Hommes.*' It must not be presented as a '*terre des nations*' or a '*terre des machines.*' "

Physical planning for Expo '67 began in the same year as the Montebello Conference, 1963. Initially, the team of planners hired by the exhibition corporation proposed that the fair be located within the city of Montreal. As part of this proposal, experimental housing projects were to be built in various derelict areas of the city, hopefully to act as catalysts for future revitalization.

But poor and run-down urban areas were not part of the successful and exciting image of Montreal that Mayor Jean Drapeau wanted to project to the rest of the world. Instead, Drapeau proposed that the fair be located on an island in Montreal's harbour, Ile Sainte-Hélène. When it became apparent that this island alone was not large enough to accommodate the fair, a new island was created alongside, and named Ile Nôtre-Dame. Thus, the site for Expo '67 was established: isolated by water from Montreal, but with it in view, the city was to serve as a backdrop against which the fair could unfold.

Thus, planning took a very different course than it would have, had the fair been integrated into the existing city fabric. The planners severed ties with traditional urban planning and struck out on their own to create a three-dimensional organization appropriate to "an age of sophisticated technological advances." The search began, not for a "town plan," as had been the case with previous world fairs, but rather for what was termed a "framework of orientation."

As opposed to a traditional town plan, which relies on a hierarchy of *spaces*, in terms of squares and streets, to organize the environment, the planners of Expo '67 envisioned a hierarchy of *transportation systems* to organize the fair. The primary means of transportation was to be a silver express train called the "Expo Express" which would bring visitors into, through and out of the two islands in twenty minutes if they did not get off. The Expo Express stopped at only four points within the fair, points which the planners termed "nodes." The secondary system of transportation was

Figure 1. Aerial view of Expo '67, Montreal, with Ile Sainte-Hélène in the foreground and Ile Notre-Dame in the background.

to be a monorail which travelled in loops, originating and terminating at the "nodes." Significantly, the overall organization of Expo was not to be understood as the visitor walked in and through it but, rather, from above, and at a speed of forty kilometres an hour (twenty-five miles an hour) whilst seated comfortably on the mostly-elevated Expo Express.

Four theme pavilions, representing Man the Explorer, Man the Producer, Man the Provider and Man in the Community, were to be built in conjunction with the nodes, in order to further develop these points as centres of the fair. The smaller pavilions were supposed to plug-into the theme pavilions, in the best tradition of the English architecture group Archigram's "plug-in city." Participation was not obligatory but those that opted to plug-in were permitted a "choice of

Figure 2. Expo '67, Montreal, part of the transportation system with Montreal in the background.

location and environment and allowed . . . free expression." The aim was to devise a framework which would "free the individual to contribute to the pattern rather than be imprisoned by it."

As actually built, the smaller industrial and national pavilions bore only a tangential relationship to the larger theme pavilions in their general area. Sites were limited by coverage restrictions to a minimum of 40% and a maximum of 60%. There were also height limitations on some of the pavilions, according to location. In terms of architectural style or expression, there were no real limits or restrictions; architects were "asked" to "explore the possibilities of web or film-like materials stretched over bold frames or the frank assembly of mass-produced components fastened together in patternful ways . . . " (*Figures 1,2*)

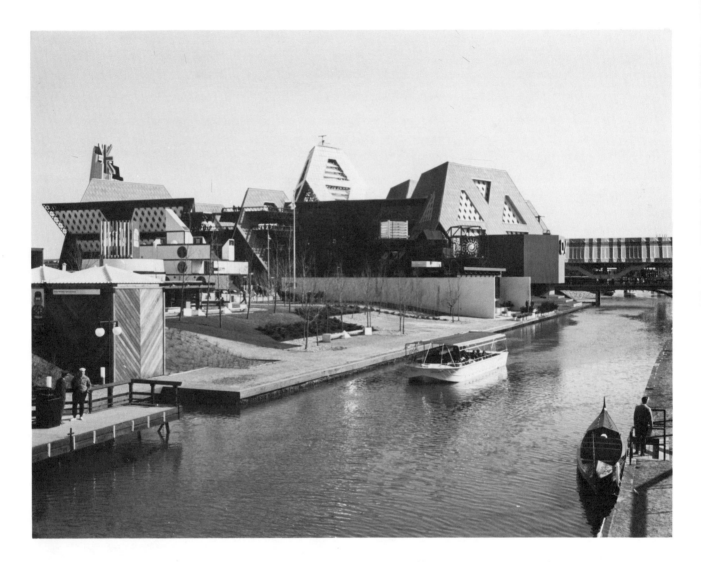

Figure 3. Expo '67, Man the Producer Pavilion, Ile Notre-Dame. Affleck Desbarats Dimakopoulos Lebensold and Sise, Architects.

Like the planners of the fair, the architects of the individual pavilions seemed intent on searching out new and experimental architectural solutions wherever possible. Man the Producer and Man the Explorer (both by Affleck, Desbarats, Dimakopoulos, Lebensold and Sise), the theme pavilions on Ile Nôtre-Dame and Ile St. Hélène respectively, were both constructed out of identically-sized tetrahedra (three-dimensional structural forms). *(Figure 3)*

The U.S. pavilion, a geodesic dome by Buckminster Fuller, was also built out of metal piping but the structure as a whole was much more complicated. In fact, the sizes and connections of metal piping required to make this "simple" geometric form were so complex that the design could be carried out only with the aid of a computer. *(Figure 4)*

The use of a computer seemed to confer a certain distinction on the designer; one architect boasted that

Figure 4. Expo '67, The United States Pavilion. Buckminster Fuller, Architect.

the structure of his pavilion was so complex that it required two hours of computer analysis, as opposed to 30,000 man-lifetimes of manual arithmetic. Apparently, pavilion design, in itself, was simply not challenging enough. The German Pavilion, in which a large, curling, steel mesh roof was hung from eight supports, could have been fifty times larger than it was without changing its design, according to Frei Otto, the architect.

Blurring the distinctions between traditional parts of buildings — between door and window, front and back, and from one room to the next — was another Expo '67 hallmark. In the German Pavilion, even the distinction between inside and outside was subtle.

To architects and non-architects alike, the fair represented a welcome departure from the boring and monotonous box-like character of modern architecture. Journalist Robert Fulford commented:

At Expo the walls slanted. Doors and windows were, quite often, not rectangular. The right angle and the straight line no longer ruled the world — there were hexagons, pentagons and truncated tetrahedrons. Not everything was made of steel and glass: there were plastics, too, and plywoods . . . . There was so much that was fresh and different and even daring that it seemed a new world of architectural design was opening up; and some of us imagined that we might even be in at the beginning of a revolution.

Architects, and especially architectural critics, were not always as willing to whole-heartedly endorse the "anything-goes" approach to the environment represented by Expo. The editor of *Progressive Architecture*, Jan Rowan, coined the phrase "no-space spaces" to describe the oft-repeated sensation, once inside many of the pavilions, of total darkness relieved only by the light of a spotlight or film projector.

"Besides no-space spaces," commented Rowan in an editorial on Expo, "what an architect will notice at Expo . . . is the discontinuity of experience." To many visitors, this very feeling was part of the overall excitement which was to be expected at a world's fair. But to many architects and planners, anxious about the increasing discontinuity between one modern building and the next (something which was especially noticeable in an urban context), the fair represented a dangerous tendency of modern architecture.

Previewing the Expo construction site in 1966, architectural critic Peter Collins wrote:

> If Canada had really wanted to give a lead in planning its celebration of Canadian unity, it might profitably have empowered the Chief Architect of Expo '67 to impose complete co-ordination in the design of each pavilion and, consequently, in the detailed design of the spaces and relationships between them. . . . I would have infinitely preferred a totally integrated environment to the

disparate miscellany which the partly-finished carcases portend.

A year before the fair had opened, Professor Collins had noted not only the eventual unrelatedness of the Expo environment but also the unusual way that Canada had chosen to celebrate its hundredth birthday. Not that having the exposition to mark the event was unusual; the United States had done the same thing in Philadelphia on its centennial in 1876 and many of the world's fairs have marked one type of anniversary or another. What was unusual was that, unlike previous fairs, and Expo '70 in Osaka, Canada played down Expo as a specifically Canadian event in favour of stressing that which all men (as opposed to nations) shared in common: Man the Producer; Man the Explorer etc. The Canadian Pavilion, which might in other circumstances have been the centrepiece of the fair, was placed off at one end of Ile Nôtre-Dame, overshadowed by the "universal" theme pavilions and other national pavilions with more presence. Rather than distinguishing Canada as a nation, from other nations, the fair proved that Canadians were just like everyone else. Put another way, Canada was just as *modern* as anyplace else. On opening day, journalist Peter Newman wrote:

> The cannonade of fireworks which marked the opening of Expo may in retrospect turn out to have been one of those rare moments that change the direction of a nation's history . . . surely the modernization of Canada — of its skylines, of its styles, its institutions — will be dated from this occasion and from this fair . . . .

Eager to shed its isolated and provincial image, Canada utilized its centennial to thrust itself into the realm of international achievement, culture and architecture. The mood was one of optimism, expansiveness and the then-pleasant sensation of flux and change.

II A Common Denominator: Mainstream Architecture in Evolution

Figure 5 The Lorne Building, designed as an office building, became the controversial "temporary" shelter for the nation's art collection for over thirty years.

Almost ten years after Expo '67, the opportunity to monumentalize another important centennial gave rise to a design competition for a new National Gallery of Canada. Sponsored by the federal Department of Public Works on the basis of a programme prepared by the National Gallery and endorsed by the National Capital Commission, the competition symbolized the exhaustion of the inventive spirit that had characterized the earlier Montreal exposition.

Like other architectural competitions, the 1976/77 National Gallery competition was intended to elicit a variety of innovative proposals for a specific building, and to choose the best among them. Not unlike the planning and design process for Expo '67, the competition was viewed as a means of creating popular and professional support for a cultural event of national importance. To understand why the agencies involved were unable to implement the winning design is to understand some of the complex factors underlying the evolution of mainstream architecture in Canada. A brief overview of these factors, insofar as they bear upon this one building — perhaps the most important public architectural commission in Canada since World War II — is a necessary introduction to the story of how the National Gallery came to be built by other agencies and other architects a decade later between 1983 and 1988, instead of by those involved in the 1976 competition.

Since it opened its doors to the public on March 13, 1880, the National Gallery has been the subject of intense if often inconclusive speculation. In those days, the Gallery collection was housed in rooms of the Clarendon Hotel, a Confederation-era building owned by the federal government. In the twentieth century, several locations and dozens of architects were considered for a building that would house the nation's art collection. The list of sites and architects constitutes a virtual pocket history of capital-area planning and national architectural trends. Among those architectural designers and advisors whose names are associated with proposals for the Gallery were Frank Darling, Percy Nobbs, Sherlock Mathers, Eric Arthur, the French architect Jacques Greber, American architects Eero Saarinen and I.M. Pei, and most recently Barton Myers, the late Ron Thom, Arthur Erickson and Peter Rose. During the Gallery's first hundred years of existence, over ten locations were designated for the institution's flagship building.

The first design competition for the building in 1952 followed on the heels of the milestone Massey-Lévesque Royal Commission on the Arts which, among its recommendations for national cultural initiatives, urged that the National Gallery be housed in a purpose-built facility.

Eric Arthur, the eminent educator, editor and proponent of modern architecture, was appointed Professional Advisor to the Gallery. Arthur called together a jury of architects known for their commitment to modern design: Alfred Barr Jr. (then Director of the Museum of Modern Art in New York), John Bland (then Director of a progressive architectural program at McGill University), and the internationally renowned architect Eero Saarinen. The competition finalists submitted designs entirely consistent with post-war International Modern architecture.

After a prolonged selection process involving a change of site and a forty per cent reduction of Eric Arthur's original programme of required spaces, the Winnipeg firm of Green, Blankstein, Russell was named the winner in 1954. Their design was a spare rectangular building with a pronounced structural frame, extensive glass panels, and an austere outdoor courtyard. Of the proposal, the jury reported that it would "weather the changing tastes of time and fashion, and that it will be a real contribution to the architecture of the Capital, and a building of which Canada can be proud."

Unconvinced by this rather trite judgment, the National Planning Commission criticized the radical style and extensive glass wall areas of the design. Responsible for the site approvals in the Capital area, the Commission expressed its dissatisfaction with the result of the three-year long competition by announcing that the site for the Gallery was to be changed to Cartier Square. The government then asked Green, Blankstein, Russell to design interior spaces in the Lorne Building, an eight-storey office block at the corner of Elgin and Slater Streets in downtown Ottawa. Although designed for government office use, the Lorne Building was designated the temporary shelter for the nation's art collection, pending construction of the competition-winning scheme on the adjacent Cartier Square. (*Figure 5*)

The move into the office building did not go smoothly. During Vincent Massey's dedication of the cornerstone, part of the building's construction hoarding collapsed, injuring four pedestrians. The unplanned-for high humidity levels required to prevent deterioration of art works caused the Lorne Building itself to deteriorate. Leaks, drafts, and even frost created an intolerable environment inside, and the exterior masonry cladding had to be replaced to avoid further building damage or injury to passersby. Soon after the Gallery's 'temporary' move into the office building, the government announced it could not justify expenditure on a new Gallery building.

When, in anticipation of the Gallery's 1980 centennial, the Department of Public Works organized a second architectural competition for the National Gallery, it went

Figure 6 Proposal by Arthur Erickson Associates with David Boulva Cleve to the 1976/77 competition for the National Gallery, aerial view of the model.

Figure 7 Proposal by Raymond Moriyama, Architects & Planners, to the 1976/77 competition for the National Gallery, aerial view of the model.

to great lengths to address the sometimes disparate objectives of the various agencies governing museum administration, siting in the nation's capital, and its own programme of federal building construction. Guy Desbarats, former partner of Affleck, Desbarats, Dimakopoulos and Sise, a Montreal architectural firm that had achieved national prominence through competition victories for the National Arts Centre in Ottawa and Place des Arts in Montreal, was at that time Assistant Deputy Minister of Public Works. For Desbarats the key aspect of the 1976 competition process was not design innovation, as it had been in Arthur's 1952 competition, but the avoidance of controversy between the government and a cost-conscious public. By his own admission, "it was more important to give work to the good firms who had already proven their design capacity . . . good track record in both management and financial control, particularly in financial control, was very necessary."

As a result of this emphasis, the Public Works' competition met with strenuous opposition from the architectural profession. The editors of *The Canadian Architect* submitted a letter of protest, signed by over eight hundred architects across Canada, to Prime Minister Trudeau, the leader of the Opposition, and Public Works officials. *Canadian Architect*'s November 1976 issue was devoted to the controversy. Despite the protest, the first stage of the competition proceeded as Public Works intended. Of 456 firms who indicated interest in the competition, only fifty-six replied to the brochure outlining the selection process. The stringent first prequalifying stage screened out the young and unproven, leaving ten mega-teams made of eighteen architectural firms, each with a full complement of engineering, cost, and, in some cases, art consultants. Not surprisingly, eight of these firms had appeared on a short-list drawn up by Public Works before the decision to hold a more open competition had been made.

Undoubtedly the most contentious aspect of the 1976 competition was the programme, an eight-hundred-page-long document that set out inflexible requirements for every aspect of the design work, from pedestrian rights-of-way to the black and white panel format. The degree of detail in the competition brief was intended to emphasize the cost restrictions for the eventual building. However, the complex demands of the programme, set against the $35,000 fee each team received for their submission, guaranteed financial sacrifice for all except the successful competitor. Blake Millar, whose team submitted one of the most innovative proposals at the end of the second stage, claimed that he had personally logged over sixteen hundred hours in the four-month time period of the competition. (On a daily basis, Millar's

estimate works out to over thirteen hours per day, not allowing for a single day off.) "It was a matter of almost total isolation to organize all the facets of the work and bring it all together," he related. "At a normal hourly rate for salary, we certainly would have logged well over $200,000 worth of time and were paid $35,000 to include all expenses."

John C. Parkin, whose firm eventually won the competition, characterized the competitors as a "group of highly competitive people, all of whom are very close friends . . . and were among the pioneers of the post-War period of buildings in Canada." Tensions among these friends, however, ran high during and long after the event.

For the National Gallery, which had prepared that part of the programme describing the spatial requirements (the document underwent subsequent refinements under the supervision of the National Capital Commission), the most contentious aspect of the 1976 competition was perhaps the choice of site. Dr. Jean Sutherland Boggs, the Gallery's Director from 1966 to 1976, had made clear her preference for the Cartier Square site recommended many years earlier by Jacques Gréber and in the wake of the 1952-54 competition by the National Capital Commission. Instead, the Department of Public Works chose a site on the west end of Wellington Street between the Supreme Court and the National Library. Briefly considered as a suitable location for the Gallery after World War I, the site had since acquired a steam heating plant with a prominent exhaust stack on its river frontage, blemishing the lone natural feature of an area of some remoteness from downtown activity. With what might be seen in retrospect as acute political pragmatism, Jean Boggs accepted an academic post at Harvard and left the Gallery a scant five weeks before the competition jury arrived in Ottawa.

Of the designs produced in these chaotic and discouraging circumstances, few demonstrated the formal inventiveness typically associated with major competitions. Sensing the uncertain outcome and conforming to the straitjacket of graphic requirements, all but a few of the entries were cautious, almost indistinguishably featureless designs, buildings intended to be innocuous backgrounds for the nation's art collection. The schemes of the senior competitors in particular displayed the tendency of mainstream architecture to reduce all buildings to a rational expression of their construction system — as if to reassure competition sponsors of the ultimate feasibility of the designs. (*Figures 6, 7, 8, 9, 10*)

For John C. Parkin, whose firm won the competition with the most structurally rhetorical scheme within this genre, the triumph of understatement confirmed his belief that design, especially as an expression of personal or stylistic character, is irrelevant to mainstream architecture. Indeed, Parkin's firm worked in the self-effacing role of local "executive architects" for pioneering Modern design architects Viljo Revell and Mies van der Rohe for the construction of Toronto City Hall and the Toronto-Dominion Centre. Parkin himself has made a veritable credo of his disavowal of a stylistic imprimatur, claiming that:

> Architects should be relatively anonymous people, working and doing a good job for people. We have to refine, and avoid digressions that are just fashions created by editors' need for cult figures. Canadians don't need a Man of the Year.

The Parkin scheme, itself the result of an in-house competition amongst staff designers, standardized the relationship of galleries to circulation spaces by imposing a prominent modular form on the entire complex. *(Figures 11, 12)* The galleries were cubes; the spaces dividing them were bridges carrying facilities: stairs, hallways, or electrical and mechanical ducts, as circumstance dictated. The proposal's modular order appealed to the jury, which included American architect I.M. Pei and the lesser-known Dutch architect W.G. Quist. Quist was an exponent of modular design. (The best-known examples of modular buildings, a competition scheme for Amsterdam City Hall and the Apeldoorn office complex, are the work of another Dutch architect, Herman Hertzberger *(Figure 13)*.) Another juror, Canadian art historian G. Stephen Vickers, remarked that:

> There was a very clear consensus that the Parkin Gallery was, like a set of child's blocks, easy to modify, especially in the event that the government did not want to spend the original budget. The possibility of building the Gallery seemed remote by the time the competition was judged, and Parkin's was the easier design to amend. It was in fact like a marriage: one was hopeful that it could change to improve.

Figure 8 Proposal by Victor Prus, Architect & Urbanist (with Bland Lemoyne Shine Lacroix, Architectes et Urbanistes and Longpre Marchand Goudreau Dobush Stewart Hein and Hebert Lalonde, Architectes) to the 1976/77 competition for the National Gallery, aerial view of the model.

Figure 9 Proposal by Clifford Wiens & Associates/Marani Rounthwaite Dick to the 1976/77 competition for the National Gallery, aerial view of the model.

Figure 10 Proposal by the Webb Zerafa Menkes Housden Partnership to the 1976/77 competition for the National Gallery, aerial view of the model.

Figure 11 The Parkin Partnership won the 1976/77 competition for the National Gallery with a neutral, modular design.

While the 1976 competition's sponsors had succeeded in eliciting an accurate survey of mainstream architecture in Canada, they were, as Vickers had foreseen, unable to sustain the necessary momentum to carry the project to construction. Shortly after the jury issued its report, commending the "subtle, unassertive, and rational" approach of the Parkin proposal, Secretary of State John Roberts announced that construction of the Gallery "would have to be reviewed in light of current fiscal restraints."

The intervening six-year period — during which a Conservative government was elected and defeated and the Liberals under Trudeau reinstated — produced a remarkable restructuring of the client agency for the National Gallery's construction project. The Trudeau government announced through an Order-in-Council in February 1982 that Jean Boggs was giving up her post as Director of the Philadelphia Museum of Art (where she had gone after teaching at Harvard) to return to Ottawa to head a special crown corporation. The Canada Museums Construction Corporation, as it was named, had as its prime mandates to recommend sites and architects and to supervise the design and construction of the National Gallery and the National Museum of Man. Boggs, whose contract as Chairman and Chief Executive Officer was terminated in May 1986 when a new Conservative government disbanded the C.M.C.C. and returned control of both construction projects to the Department of Public Works, remains convinced that the creation of the crown corporation made it possible for her to "exercise moral force with respect to the architecture. The government would never have been able to realize this (buidling) without the C.M.C.C. It's simply too hard to drive fast in a large department."

Born in Peru of Canadian parents in 1922, Jean Boggs has been hailed as Canada's "foremost internationally recognized, practising art historian." She studied with painter Arthur Lismer in Montreal from 1942 to 1944, going on to earn her Ph.D. in fine arts at Harvard. Her professional appointment at Harvard (1976-1979) and subsequent Directorship of the Philadelphia Museum of Modern Art — she is the first Canadian to hold such a position at a major American museum — gave her the administrative stature needed, in addition to her extensive professional credentials, to head the C.M.C.C. As Director of the National Gallery (1966-1976), she had campaigned strenuously to achieve a home for the chronically ill-accommodated institution. She had also witnessed, without ultimately presiding over, the preparations for the second abandoned architectural competition.

This experience proved essential to the selection of sites and architects for the National Gallery and the Museum of Civilization. Eschewing the time-consuming preparations of an open national architectural competition, Boggs quickly and discreetly consulted a vast number of architects, government officials, deans of architectural schools, architectural critics, and competition organizers in a wide-ranging search for firms with exceptional design experience.

Challenged by the national professional association that the selection process contravened standards for choosing architects, Boggs defended her role as both a politically and architecturally necessary one. She contended that other competitions, such as that for the Mississauga City Hall or for National Galleries past, had produced designs conceived to reflect the predilections of the strongest architect on the jury.

> It is harder to guess the nature of the judgement to be made with someone like me . . . I think there are fewer commitments perhaps with someone like me than with someone who has devoted his whole life to architecture like (James) Stirling (juror, Mississauga City Hall competition). My criteria are intuitive, certainly, and one could say, less committed to one particular point of view or one

particular school . . . When (I.M.) Pei was chosen for the East Wing, it was just the decision of the Board and the Director of the National Gallery (in Washington, D.C.) . . . Historically it works. Urban VIII was right when he chose Bernini.

Within twelve months of her appointment, Boggs had reviewed sites, screened over ninety architectural candidates, conducted two closed design competitions, and announced the final selections, approved by Cabinet, of sites and architects for both museums. The final selection, however, took the five competitors for the Gallery's Ottawa (and thus Ontario) site by surprise. Moshe Safdie, in association with the Quebec firm of Desnoyers, Mercure, had submitted a proposal for the Museum of Civilization to be sited in Hull, Quebec across the river from the Gallery, but was appointed architect for the National Gallery. Parkin Partnership's Toronto office, which had not been short-listed at all by Boggs but which had won the 1976 competition, was joint-ventured with Safdie for the commission in place of Desnoyers, Mercure. Douglas J. Cardinal Architect, who had like

Figure 12 Presentation panel from the Parkin Partnership's proposal showing Systems Integration.

CANADIAN GALLERIES
EUROPEAN & AMERICAN GALLERIES
MODERN & CONTEMPORARY GALLERIES

COMPETITOR'S NO.:
4567890123

PROJECT :
LIMITED ARCHITECTURAL COMPETITION
NEW NATIONAL GALLERY OF CANADA

DRAWING :
SYSTEMS INTEGRATION

DRAWING NO.
20

Figure 13 Amsterdam Town Hall Competition proposal, Herman Hertzberger. Aerial view of the model.

Safdie been invited to submit a proposal for the Museum of Civilization, was appointed architect for that museum in association with a Quebec firm hitherto uninvolved in the selection process.

The C.M.C.C.'s Advisory Board is credited with the reshuffling of the joint ventures. Made up of Cabinet appointees without affiliations to departments, as well as of high-ranking officials from the departments of Public Works and the National Capital Commission, the Advisory Board played a key political role in the selection process. According to a Gallery administrator involved in the project:

> Aspects of design in the proposals certainly made some architects front-runners. But the Liberal Cabinet had made it clear that it wanted to have a greater role in the selection than it normally would. The Deputy Ministers had a major impact. The National Capital Commission felt Safdie was more sensitive to site issues than those who had been asked to submit proposals for the National Gallery. Public Works wanted the commitment to Parkin from the 1976 competition honoured. The Cabinet appointees — Hyman Soloway from Ottawa and the architect Jean Issalys from Hull — could express themselves freely, without being concerned about schedule or budget constraints.

Architects who participated in the unofficial 1982 competition for the National Gallery had been forewarned that the invitation was to demonstrate "a measure of your imagination and not a design" and that architects asked to submit ideas for the Museum might be considered for the Gallery, and vice versa. For his part, Moshe Safdie was not displeased by the cross-appointment or the last-minute switch in joint-venture partners. Although reported to have been reassigned to the National Gallery's picturesque site on Major's Hill Park in part because of his sensitivity to the Hull site during the competition, Safdie recalls that his design for the Museum of Man had made the National Capital Commission "very nervous, because of the stairs descending into the river interrupting the park." His Museum scheme, while similar to his earlier projects for the Musée National de la Civilisation in Quebec City or the San Francisco State College, was to have no visible relationship to the design he was later to present for the National Gallery.

Born in 1938 in Israel, Safdie began his career as an architect in Montreal with the internationally renowned Habitat building for Expo '67. Since that precocious debut (Safdie was in his late twenties when the project was built), his commissions and academic appointments have been primarily outside Canada. His main office, which has been responsible for the National Gallery project, is in Massachusetts within commuting distance to Harvard University, where he directed the Urban Design Program from 1978 until 1985. In 1981, he won the competition of the Musée National de la Civilisation in Quebec. The National Gallery therefore is his third building commission in Canada, and his second national cultural institution within a two-year time frame.

Safdie relished the challenge of working with Boggs on the National Gallery, although he claims "it was a tougher site than the Museum of Man, a site full of contradictions. The Gallery had to be positioned at the end, in the park; the entrance had to be at the corner, on Sussex." In the initial stages he scrutinized the site, and toured a variety of buildings and public spaces in Rome, Florence, Milan, Munich, Stuttgart, Cologne, and London with Boggs and other Gallery officials in order to familiarize himself with the architectural predilections of his client. As well, Safdie studied the submissions of the five firms that had originally been asked to make Gallery proposals. "Barton Myers' scheme was the best," concluded Safdie of the schemes. "The entry and approach to the galleries particularly were good." (*Figure 14*)

His own approach to the Gallery's design was to prepare two alternative schemes for Cabinet approval, as he had done earlier with his Museum of Civilization proposal. One scheme featured an interior colonnaded public courtyard, entered from Sussex Drive and lined on its two lateral sides by galleries. The "introvert" scheme, as it was dubbed by Safdie, was favoured by Gallery curators, who felt it offered optimal access to gallery spaces from the primary public area. The rival "extrovert" scheme, similar to the Barton Myers Associates proposal, brought visitors through a spectacular long, glass-enclosed porch that faced Major's Hill Park and led to a Great Hall, from which the galleries could be reached. "The Cabinet committee was split 3/3," recalled Safdie. Francis Fox, then Minister of Communications, admired the "extrovert" design with its vast glass facade facing beyond Major's Hill to Parliament, calling it a "sparkling jewel." Boggs, for her part, had been won over to the "extrovert" scheme for its knowing reference to Italian architectural precedents. " In the end," Safdie said, "Trudeau himself decided. It was to be the extrovert."

Figure 14 Barton Myers Associates' proposal for the National Gallery, made in 1983 to the Canada Museums Construction Corporation, was admired by Moshe Safdie, who was awarded the commission although his firm had participated in the parallel competition for the Museum of Civilization. Aerial view of the model.

Figure 15 Model of Moshe Safdie's design for the National Gallery: view from the southeast with the Roman Catholic Basilica in the lower right and the War Museum behind the Gallery along Sussex Drive.

Figure 16 View of the Safdie design model from above the tower of the La Salle Academy. The War Museum is seen to to the right of the landscaped court. Canadian, European and American Galleries are to the left of the court; Modern and Contemporary Galleries are in the wing with bay window facing the court.

Figure 17 Detail of the model showing the Great Hall, a granite-clad concrete and glass homage to the Parliamentary Library.

In developing the "extrovert" scheme, Safdie has designed a Gallery that, although it advances some themes from his earlier buildings, represents a direction for his architecture that may surprise those who are familiar with his work and written statements. The building is not based on a systematic clustering of constructed components (as in Habitat, or his joint-venture partner's earlier modular Gallery), as much as it is an assembly of different building fragments, some of which overtly recall other buildings of importance to the history of architecture. *(Figure 15)* Some of those buildings are to be found in the Gallery's immediate context. The glazed entrance pavilion of the new Gallery is located on Sussex Drive (an important ceremonial route in the Capital, leading to both the Prime Minister's and the Governor-General's residences); in its scale and shape it refers to the tower of the La Salle Academy across Sussex, while its lightly reflective glass and stone-clad frame set it apart as a contemporary construction. A landscaped court to the north of the entrance and the Canadian, European, and American gallery wing reveals the south facade of the baronial style War Museum. (*Figure 16*) Toward the heavily wooded Nepean Point at the western edge of the site, the building culminates in the Great Hall, a super-

Figure 18 Rendering by Michael Guran of the glazed, ramped walkway leading to the Great Hall. Visible through the glass panels are towers of the Parliament Buildings and the conical roof of the Library.

Figure 19 Construction photograph illustrating the relationship of the Colonnade, which leads to the Great Hall, to the Parliamentary Library.

scale version of the entrance pavilion and a recognizable homage to the Parliamentary Library (designed by Thomas Fuller and H. Chilion Jones in 1859, and completed by Thomas S. Scott and John Bowes in 1877). The Great Hall is approached through a steeply proportioned, ramped hall. (*Figures 17, 18*) In much the same way that the escalators are the prime image of the Centre Pompidou in Paris, the "Scala Regia," as it is called by project personnel familiar with its Roman precedent, is both from within and without the prime image of the Gallery for the casual visitor. Through the immense sheets of glass enclosing the Great Hall at the end of the "Scala Regia,"

one looks across the Ottawa River to the delicate but opaque Victorian Gothic masonry of the Library and beyond its conical roof to the towers of the Parliament Buildings. Parliament appears to have been miniaturized, contained within the massive structural frame of the Great Hall, like a sketchbook study for the Gallery's own facade. (*Figures 19, 20, 21*)

Inside the building, the gallery spaces evoke a series of familiar, if not always local, precedents. The Canadian galleries and the European and American galleries on the floor above them occupy the largest wing of the building, running along the north edge of the Colonnade.

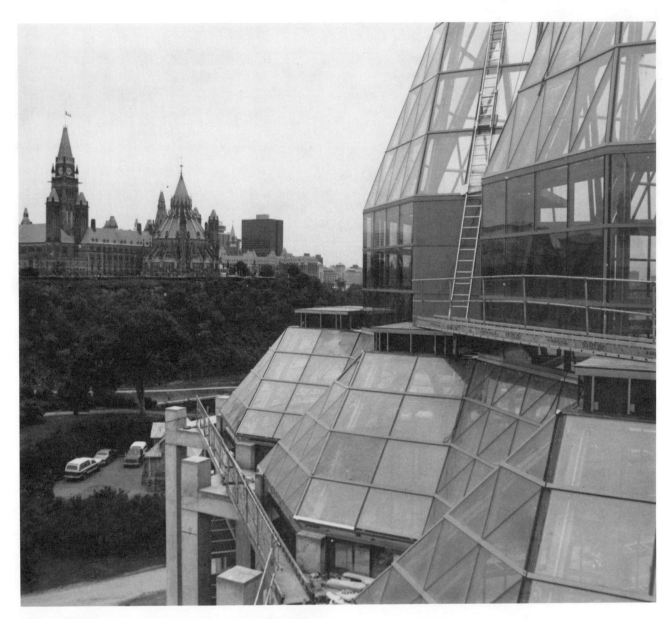

Figure 20 Construction photograph showing the faceted profile of the Great Hall in relationship to the conical form of the Parliamentary Library.

Figure 21 Construction photograph taken inside the Great Hall looking over Major's Hill Park toward Parliament.

Figure 22 Plan of the first floor level of the galleries. The Canadian galleries ocupy the main wing of the building, bracketed by the entrance pavilion (lower right corner) and the Great Hall (lower left corner). A skylift corridor runs north from the Great Hall to a rotunda from which one enters the restaurant on the left and the Modern and Contemporary Galleries on the right. At the top of the drawing, a bridge connects from the Gallery to its splayed administrative wing.

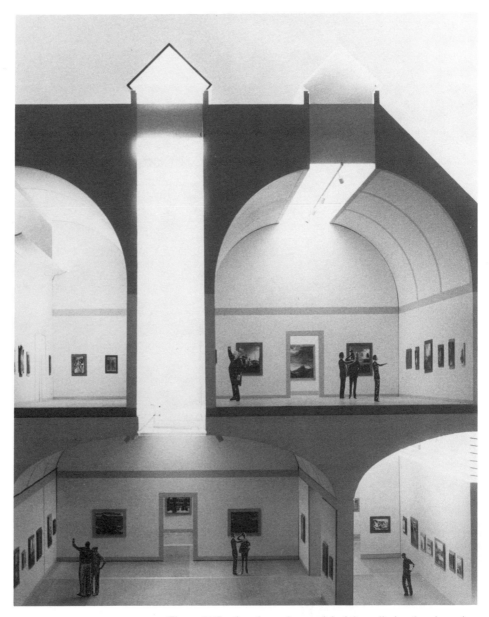

Figure 23 Section through a model of the galleries showing mirrored shafts transmitting light to Canadian galleries below.

Because the nature of the Canadian, European, and American collections is historical and therefore relatively static from a curatorial point of view, the galleries are spatially defined rather than highly flexible. (*Figure 22*) Their vaulted ceilings, with mirrored chimney-like openings admitting diffused natural light, recall the Kimbell Museum in Fort Worth, Texas (Louis I. Kahn, 1972) and the Dulwich Gallery outside of London, England (John Soane, 1813). (*Figures 23, 24*)

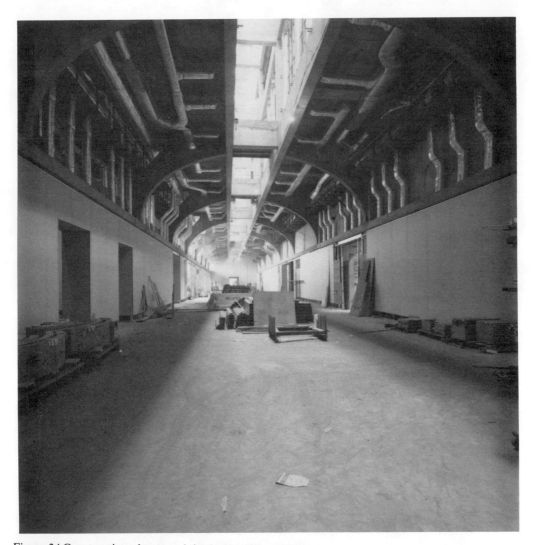

Figure 24 Construction photograph in the Canadian galleries.
The vaulted shape of the ceiling will be made of a finished
drywall ceiling suspended from, and following the curvature
of the concrete ribs.

The main wing of the Gallery is organized around
two light courts (as in another of Louis Kahn's museums,
the Yale Center for British Art), one rectangular and one
square in plan. Responding to curatorial ambivalence
about the admission of natural light in gallery spaces,
Safdie has made these courts as rooms with window-
punctuated walls, so that particular areas might be shut-
tered or blocked off to further limit the exposure of works
of art to harmful ultra-violet rays. (*Figures 25, 26*) Also
included in this wing is a restoration of the nineteenth
century chapel interior from the demolished Rideau Street
Convent (Chapel design by Canon Georges Bouillon,
1888). The Chapel's interior, rescued from demolition by

Figure 25 Rendering by Michael Guran of the Garden Court seen from the Canadian Galleries. The Rideau chapel is positioned (beyond view) behind the wall at the end.

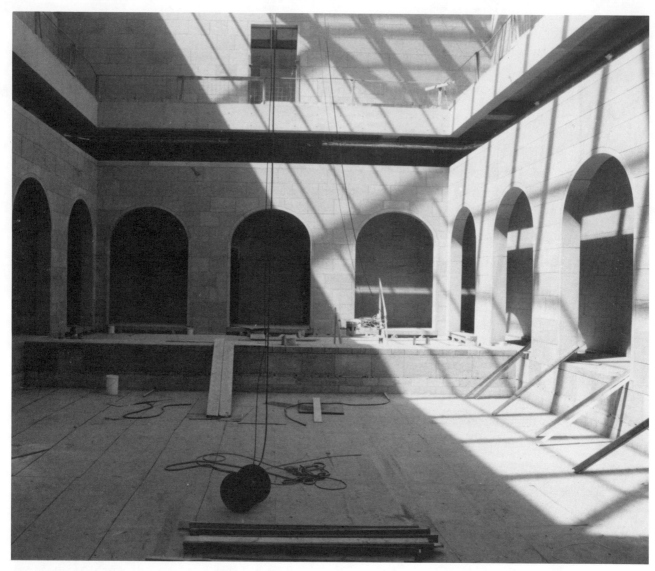

Figure 26 Construction photograph showing the Garden Court.

the Gallery, has been restored with funding from Montreal architect and patron of the arts Phyllis Lambert, and its 1100 components have been inventoried, conserved and reassembled under the direction of Parks Canada. (*Figures 27, 28, 29*) Safdie's office had responsibility for placing the restored Chapel in the larger ensemble of Canadian galleries, as its interior is an important work of Canadian art in its own right. The Rideau Chapel's interior, with its spectacular painted wood fan vaults, is embedded between the two light courts. The graceful lightness of its architecture is encased in the Canadian gallery wing with its long vaulted spaces, an accommodation that Safdie claims added an unanticipated metre and a half to the overall height of the design. As with the view of the Parliamentary Library from the Great Hall, there is a a lack of self-irony in the contrast of Gothic and contemporary spaces, a determined neutrality in the combination of local and imported architectural fragments.

As the components of the building extend northward from the prime public colonnade and the major historical

Figure 27 East-west section through the main wing of the Gallery showing the fan-vaulted Rideau chapel between two light courts.

Figure 28 Interior of the Convent of Our Lady of the Sacred Heart, formerly on the corner of Waller and Besserer Streets, Ottawa, also known as the Rideau Street Convent Chapel, 1887—1888. Archival photograph of the cast iron and painted wood fan vaults in their original state.

Figure 29 Restorers at work on the Rideau Street Convent Chapel.

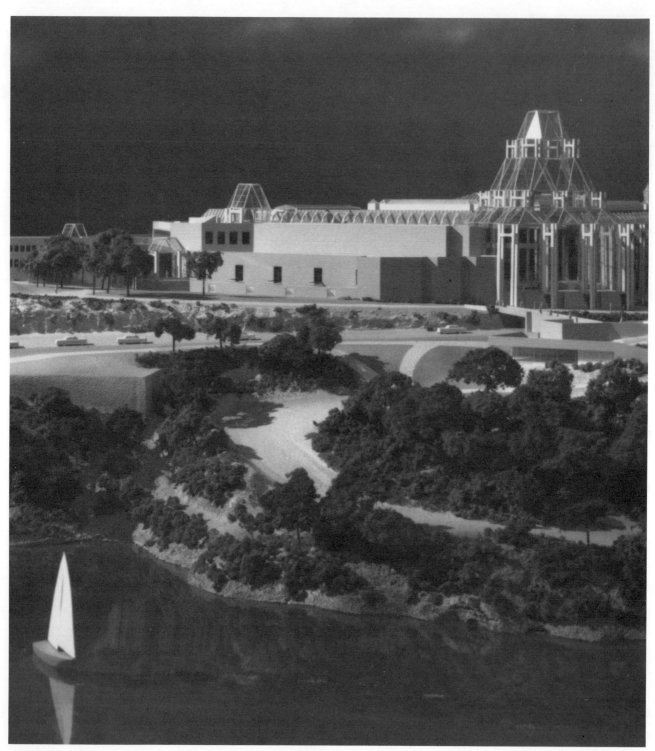

Figure 30 View of the design model from the west showing Special Exhibitions Gallery below and Prints, Drawings and Photographs above. These collections are housed in a wing that offers a largely blank terraced facade to Nepean Point.

Figure 31 Construction photograph inside the Contemporary Galleries: requirements for flexible, non-articulated, and highly controllable environments have resulted in loft-like space largely devoid of natural light.

galleries of Canadian, European and American art, they become more anonymous in character, like the "background" architecture of the 1976/77 competition entries. Because of their respective requirements for flexible, non-articulated, and highly controllable spaces, the galleries for special exhibits, for contemporary art, and for prints, drawings and photographs are conventionally framed, and with few exceptions, devoid of natural light. (*Figures 30, 31*) Skylights through the centre bay of the upper contemporary galleries have been the subject of a controversy between the architect and contemporary art curators, described by Jean Boggs in an article she has written about the Gallery's design for the *Burlington Magazine*. Structure has been provided at Safdie's insistence for skylights that the curators did not want installed. The debate belies Safdie's admiration for Louis Kahn, whom he worked for in 1962 and 1963, and whose belief that architecture is animated through natural light is antithetical to the neutral, artificially lit spaces favoured by many curators of contemporary art.

As a result of this controversy, the skylit court at the junction of the Special and Contemporary gallery wings is the smallest in area of all the courtyard spaces in the Gallery. The diminutive octagonal court signals the end of public circulation northward, as it leads to a wing of administrative and curatorial facilities inaccessible to all but Gallery-related personnel and visitors. Oriented toward the river and less monumental views of Hull and the Museum of Civilization, the administrative wing is a splayed L-shaped office building, structurally separate

Figure 32 The administrative wing viewed from the north. A small skylit bay at the bend in the administrative building aligns with the light court of the Special and Contemporary Galleries, and beyond with the Great Hall.

from the Gallery to which it is simply connected by an enclosed bridge. (*Figure 32*)

In contrast with many of the 1976/77 competition schemes, and in contrast to Safdie's own earlier projects, the design of the National Gallery emphasizes not the similarity but rather the diversity of its constituent parts. The similarities that do exist, such as the crystalline forms of the various light courts, are played down through differences in scale and in location. The dominant experience of the building is of a carefully controlled variety of forms and spaces, of rooms different in character arranged around a loose network of toplit interior courts. The dominant image of the building from the exterior is again a diversity of responses to site conditions: the grand ''sparkling jewel'' facade addressing Parliament, the utilitarian service court revealing the War Museum, the tower acknowledging the La Salle Academy, the administrative wing facing the Museum of Civilization and Hull. (*Figures 33, 34, 35*) All these disparate parts are unified

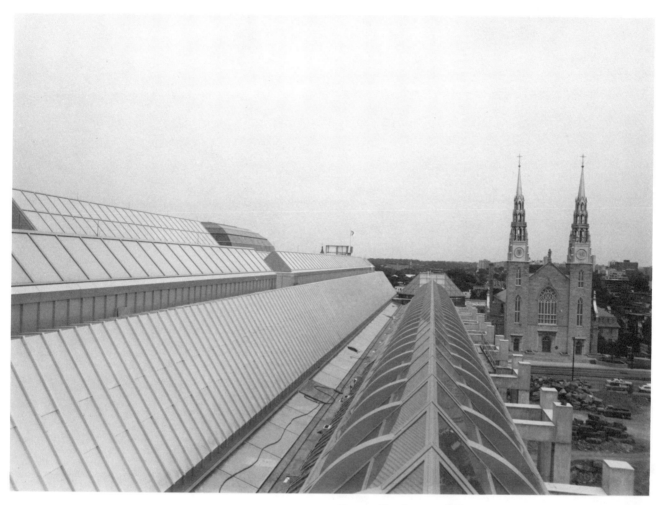

Figure 33 Construction photograph of the roof of the Colonnade.

Figure 34 Construction photograph of the concourse balcony
level of the Colonnade.

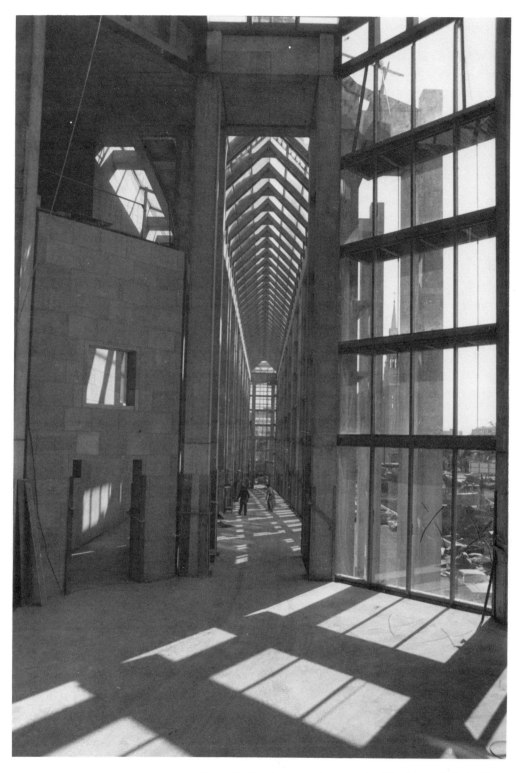

Figure 35 Construction photograph of the Great Hall, looking towards the Colonnade, the ''sparkling jewel'' facade addressing Parliament.

Figure 36 Construction photograph of the National Gallery, looking across Sussex Drive. The disparate parts of the Gallery are unified by a polished cladding of reflective glass and light pinkish grey Quebec granite, distinct from the matte limestone of neighbouring landmarks.

Figure 37 Although the ''sparkling jewel'' facade with its repetitive concrete structure and honeycomb of skylights displays aspects of modular composition, the overall building marks a moderation of the relentless, modular innovation demonstrated by Moshe Safdie in his earlier Habitat project.

by a polished cladding of light pinkish grey Quebec granite that stands out subtly from the matte limestone of Ottawa's landmarks. (*Figures 36, 37*)

Within Moshe Safdie's career, the National Gallery project marks a moderation of the radical, modular innovation demonstrated in Habitat. Although in an article entitled "Private Jokes in Public Places," Safdie criticized a number of his Ivy League colleagues for abandoning the Modern Movement's exploration of construction technologies and falling back on historical models, he has shown in the National Gallery that he can be responsive to a client's predilections for historical narrative. His alliance with architects who sought to modify, rather than to reject, Modern architecture makes his work, like that of other mainstream architects such as John C. Parkin, difficult to characterize. For Safdie's current work is consciously devoid of personal style. Unlike Douglas Cardinal, whose Museum of Civilization in Hull is a recognizable refinement of the architecture of all his previous projects, Safdie's Gallery is part of a protean process. Asked whether he felt people visiting the Gallery would recognize it as a "Safdie design," Safdie replied:

There is ambivalence for me about architecture as a personal trademark. The architects I admire most, like Louis Kahn and Frank Lloyd Wright, worked with an extreme diversity of forms. If you consider the Guggenheim Museum in New York, the Johnson's Wax Building in Michigan, and Fallingwater in Pennsylvania, these are all very different buildings but all are distinctly Wright. For me the best architects are those who are very inventive, very diverse, but in whose work there is a common denominator.

In this philosophical flexibility, Safdie found a strong ally in Jean Boggs. "It is somewhat surprising to a conventionally, transatlantically-trained art historian to discover that the architect makes no pretence to catholicity of taste," she recalled of the formative stages of the project. Safdie, she concluded, "found reinforcement for his design when he visited the Scala Regia and photographed the gradual ramp of the Corridoio del Bernini leading to it. From many sources and close collaboration with the Gallery staff his design for a new National Gallery of Canada has developed." The lack of an overriding single character for that design, which Safdie has attributed to the breakneck pace of the project, was welcomed by the "transatlantically-trained" Boggs, who has had to contend with the diverse pressures of an Advisory Board, an impending change in government, and above it all, her own unwavering determination to see the Gallery built.

III The Will to Conserve

By the time the oil crisis struck in 1973, concern for the environment had been growing in Canada as elsewhere. Pollution Probe had been founded in 1969 to monitor environmental and energy issues. In that same year, Ontario had limited the use of DDT to bat and mouse control, and the International Joint Commission, having studied the pollution in the lower Great Lakes, had advised the Canadian and U.S. governments to immediately reduce the use of phosphates to a minimum practical level. In Halifax, Toronto and Vancouver (as in New Orleans, New York and San Francisco) community groups battled against the destruction of inner city neighbourhoods and their replacement by anonymous, isolated highrises or, even worse, by the superhighways required to carry greater numbers of people between their suburban houses and downtown commercial cores.

But the oil crisis marked a real turning point. Although in Canada the crisis was at first more a matter of anxious anticipation than of real scarcity, it sparked a genuine change in attitudes towards both the natural and built environment. In the course of a post-1973 decline in the western world's economic health, notions of unlimited growth and technological progress, notions epitomized by Expo, were called into question. Where before there had been a handful of acutely perceptive critics — Jane Jacob's *The Death and Life of Great American Cities* was published in 1961, Rachel Carson's *Silent Spring*, in 1963 — and but a few, isolated, protesting citizens fearful of losing their homes and neighbourhoods, there was suddenly a whole society faced with a threat to its prosperous way of life.

Changes in Canada's political climate were also caused by a general perception that the underlying structure of Canadian society was gradually beginning to shift. A similar perception in the United States gave rise to an intellectual movement labelled Neo-Conservatism. Espousing the values of continuity and hierarchy, this U.S. movement struck a responsive chord in Canada.

Not simply a reactionary force, the new conservatism has provided the basis for a new and progressive way of looking at the environment. It has produced a number of bold and important projects which have sought to save key neighbourhoods of our cities from obscurity or destruction.

The Promenade, Halifax

When the City of Halifax proposed a cross-town expressway alongside its waterfront in the late sixties, it did so because here, it seemed, lay the path of least resistance and, hopefully, the makings of a picturesque drive. Because the expressway would have destroyed the run-down but historic, waterfront district, citizen opposition arose in response to the idea. A group calling itself the "Committee of Concern and the Heritage Trust of Nova Scotia," and including Halifax architect Allen Duffus, made a formal submission to City Council, outlining the value of the waterfront district.

The submission argued that restoration of existing buildings could be carried out without overwhelming difficulty, and it cited as precedents projects such as Bastion Square in Victoria and Old Montreal. New uses for the waterfront were proposed, many of them related to existing structures and uses. A public marina was suggested as the most obvious and simplest function with provision for indigenous maritime industries, like yacht supply and customs brokerage, as well as for tourist-related businesses. "Imaginatively restored and developed," suggested the Heritage Trust, "this complex could provide Halifax with both a reflection of its early maritime heritage and a productive enterprise in a renewed city."

The Heritage Trust appealed directly to the public with an advertisement placed in the *Halifax/Herald Mail Star*. "These buildings," explained the ad, "are an historic heritage of the citizens of Halifax and the people of Canada." The ad asked citizens to sign their names to a form which said: "Please reconsider your decision to demolish the historic waterfront buildings," and to mail it to City Hall. "The response," Allan Duffus recalls, "was unbelievable. The Mayor and City Councillors were flooded with mail and telephone calls."

Responding to public interest — the Mayor received more letters in favour of retaining the waterfront buildings than he had on any other single civic issue — City Council rescinded its earlier decision to demolish the historic buildings, and called for proposals to develop the area.

A little less than four and one-half acres in size, the historic district was one of the last remnants of Halifax's early and prosperous beginnings. Located at the City's southeastern waterfront edge, the small pocket of nineteenth-century, brick, stone and wood buildings had as neighbours the multi-block, multi-tower Scotia Square to the west, and bank towers and a new courthouse building to the south.

Two proposals were received. "Harborside 1850," submitted by Californian Robert Abbott, proposed, amongst other features, a convention centre and a lighthouse. Abbott's plan was rejected in favour of a less flamboyant proposal by Halifax developer John Fiske, who had hired Allen Duffus' architectural firm, Duffus Romans Kundzins Rounsefell, to work out the design.

The overall intent of the Duffus Romans Kundzins Rounsefell plan was to enhance the existing buildings and to knit the area together by means of a pedestrian route which would run from the waterfront westward towards Scotia Square, linking the three main segments of the historic area. The first segment was a group of seven early warehouse buildings on the water's edge. The second was a block, on the east side of Granville Street, of commercial buildings (1859-63) destined to contain "The Promenade." And the third was a block of buildings on the west side of Granville Street, planned for redevelopment as a hotel. This block was to be connected to the Scotia Square development by a pedestrian walkway. *(Figures 41, 42)*

Duffus offered a "restoration philosophy" as the basis for his firm's design. The nineteenth-century identity of the buildings would be conserved and serviced to meet modern-day needs, while the nineteenth-century character of the open spaces would be maintained and enhanced by the use of street furniture, paving and landscaping. The whole area was to be developed as a "pedestrian precinct," with automobile access limited to service vehicles; and as an "historic precinct," a self-contained community that would not only attract visitors and tourists but also would be a pleasant place to live and work. Duffus' proposal was able to go ahead when the Nova Scotia College of Art and Design and Parks Canada agreed to rent space in the revitalized district. The College was especially supportive, committing itself as a tenant in the project for the next thirty-four years.

The Halifax waterfront restoration was completed in 1981. It can be best understood, like most architectural projects, by touring the area on foot. Starting at the water's edge, it soon becomes apparent that the restoration of the waterfront warehouses and the addition of the three new ones has been largely but not entirely successful. The buildings comprising this area's extraordinary architectural heritage — the Privateer's Warehouse (c.1810), where goods "legally" pirated from enemy ships were stored until they could be sold at public auction, and the Collins Bank and Warehouse (1825), the first private bank in Nova Scotia — have

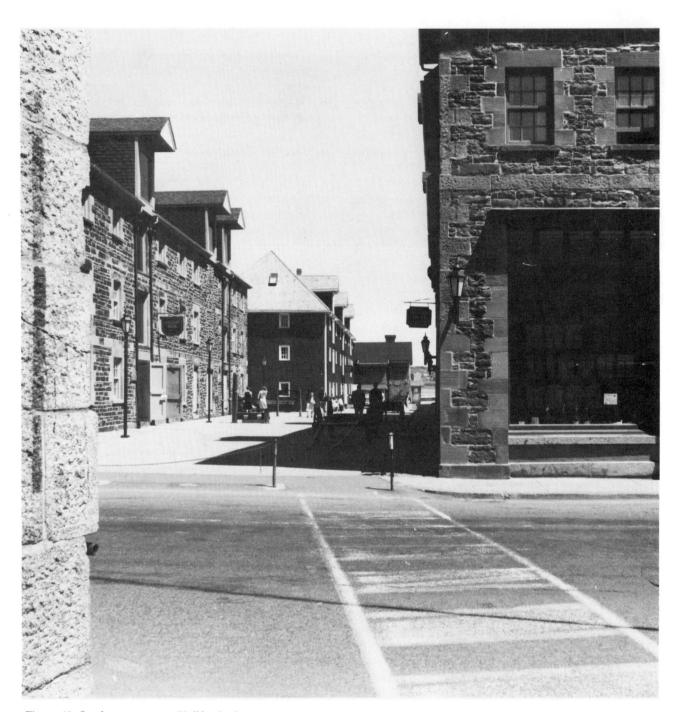

Figure 41. Outdoor square on Halifax harbour.

Figure 42. Halifax waterfront district, Site plan. Duffus Romans Kundzins Rounsefell, Architects.

been carefully rehabilitated. Their nineteenth-century seaside flavour remains intact.

It is in the addition of the new buildings, and in the use of the spaces between buildings to create two new areas, that this segment of the Halifax restoration has had mixed results. The first of these new areas is an outdoor square fashioned from a previously-unused space between two parallel warehouses. The second is an entirely new indoor mall which is defined on one side by an old warehouse and on the other by a new row of shops.

The outdoor square is a vibrant place. With sound bouncing off stone walls and salt in the air, it offers views of the harbour and casually-arranged seating places.

Figure 43. Indoor mall, Halifax harbour. Duffus Romans Kundzins Rounsefell, Architects.

The indoor mall, on the other hand, is somewhat anonymous in character. Although its spaciousness, abundant natural light and exposed, barn-like structure make it an attractive place, the *place*, by and large, could be anywhere. Entry is gained only by the doors at either end and, once inside, views to the surrounding area and particularly to the harbour are severed. The inward-looking character of the mall inevitably has had an effect on the adjacent harbourfront land, where no special provision has been made, either for walking or sitting, for visitors to the water's edge. *(Figure 43)*

Uphill and inland from the waterfront warehouses is Granville Street, historically one of the most important commercial streets of Halifax. A great fire swept through the street in 1859 and, according to a contemporary account in the *London Illustrated News,* "Houses and stores, wooden, brick, and stone alike, fed the flames until . . . sixty of the finest buildings in Halifax . . . were destroyed." Following the fire, one of Canada's largest architecture firms, William Thomas and Sons, was chosen to redesign what the London paper would later term "the Haligonian's Paradise":

Granville Street.

The result was an energetic row of four-storey buildings. At street level, elegant glass and iron store-fronts enticed those passing by with luxurious displays. Above, facades of multicoloured brick and stone, with windows capped by round and pointed arches, made reference to Venetian Gothic, Romanesque, and Italian Renaissance architecture. Characteristic of Thomas' style, as also evidenced in the Don Jail in Toronto, sculptured masks — some comical, others highly serious — look out from their positions atop many of the block's windows. *(Figures 44, 45)*

By clearing out the block's former service area, a two-level promenade running parallel to Granville and Hollis Streets was created. Logically called "The Promenade," its two levels are enclosed by a new roof of heavy timbers interspersed with skylights. Two former shops, one on Granville, the other on Hollis, have been used to provide entrances and lobbys to The Promenade, creating a graceful transition between the old street and the new promenade.

Figures 44,45. The eastern side of Granville Street, Halifax. Thomas & Sons, Original Architects; Duffus Romans Kundzins Rounsefell, Restoration.

The Granville Street entrance is marked by a canvas canopy and leads to a clean, white vestibule well-lit by its glass front to the street. To the left is a small plaque reading "The Nova Scotia College of Art and Design," and a locked door, slim evidence of the presence of the College in the warehouse space above the stores. From this vestibule, one continues towards The Promenade itself, through a doorway flanked by Corinthian columns and capped by a Moorish-style arch. *(Figure 46)*

Through the arch and another smaller vestibule, perpendicular to the visitor's line of entry, is the upper, skylit level of The Promenade. Entry from Hollis Street, on the other side of the block, brings one into The Promenade's lower, crypt-like level. Upper and lower levels merge in a provocative, multi-levelled space, a powerful focus for The Promenade and therefore the whole carefully-rehabilitated waterfront district of Halifax.

Figure 46. A former Granville Street shop made into a vestibule of The Promenade, Halifax. Duffus Romans Kundzins Rounsefell, Architects.

Figure 47. The Promenade, Halifax. Restored cast-iron columns with gold-painted capitals.

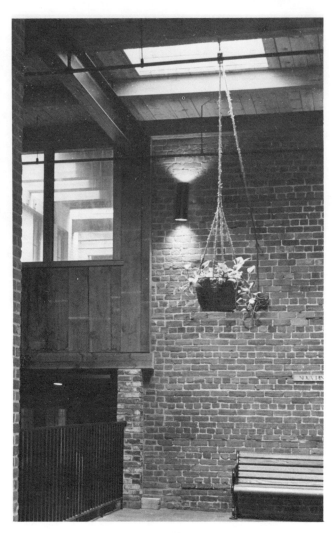

Figure 48. The Promenade, Halifax, Multi-levelled central space. Duffus Romans Kundzins Rounsefell, Architects.

Figure 49. Skylights and carefully placed windows provide unusual views out of The Promenade.

From this central space, one can see back out through the stores on both levels to the street. The backs of the stores have been replaced by glass, and cast-iron Corinthian columns have been retained, their shafts painted black and capitals gold. Skylights above the upper level reveal the backs of the Hollis Street buildings rising above, enticing a comparison between identical windows, some now inside, some still outside. *(Figures 47, 48, 49)*

The block on the western side of Granville Street, the final third of the initial master plan, has been partially restored, but mostly rebuilt as Barrington Place Inn, by the architects Page and Steele. It is now a 200-room hotel with stores on the lower levels. The renovation of this block is in some ways clever, but it is more successful on the outside than it is on the inside.

Although the facades of this four storey block were, where possible, retained, the inside of the block was completely gutted and replaced by a new concrete structure and brand new interior. Interestingly enough, because of the extent of the work on the interior, the facades had to be disassembled stone-by-stone, numbered and replaced onto the face of the "new building" in the same painstaking manner.

A new, fifth storey was added to the block in the form of a steeply-pitched mansard roof set back from the face of the restored facades. It is an addition which is skillful and sensitive to the proportions and feel of the existing exterior. Ultimately, however, this carefully renovated exterior gives way to a modern, "international" hotel interior which lacks the interest and regional character of The Promenade across the street.

Sussex Drive Redevelopment, Ottawa

Like The Promenade, the Sussex Drive Redevelopment project in Ottawa reflects a recent trend towards re-use of what were yesterday's service spaces, hidden from view in the middle of buildings or whole blocks. The project was born in 1961 when the National Capital Commission (N.C.C.) received Cabinet approval to acquire and preserve four blocks of heritage commercial buildings (1850-1870) along Sussex Drive. The intent at the time was simply to preserve the buildings from demolition and in 1964 the Sussex Drive facades were cleaned, repaired and painted.

By 1970, the plans of the N.C.C. for the area had gone beyond that of mere preservation, perhaps due in part to the appointment of Arthur Capling as Chief Architect. In hope of creating an alternative to the formal and ceremonial nature of Sussex Drive, which is the main boulevard leading from Parliament Hill to the prime minister's residence, the governor-general's residence, Rideau Hall, and Rockcliffe Park, the N.C.C. embarked on a programme of restoring the internal courts of the four blocks along Sussex Drive which it owned. Up until this time, these spaces were used for deliveries, storage and parking. *(Figure 50)*

Figure 50. Sussex Drive Redevelopment project, Ottawa, Site plan. From right to left: Clarendon Court, York Court, Place Jeanne d'Arc, Tin House Court. National Capital Commission, Arthur Capling, Chief Architect.

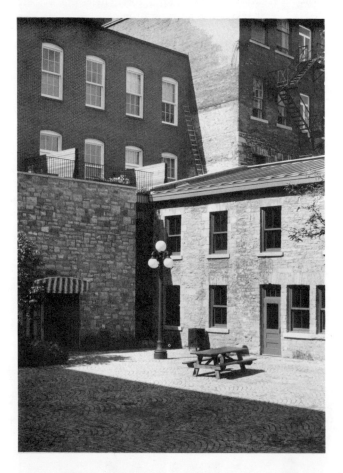

Partially completed by 1979, the idiosyncratic and picturesque nature of these former service spaces is emphasized by the casual placement of fountains, trees, benches, and sculpture against the two- to four-storey brick and stone nineteenth-century buildings. Art galleries, restaurants and shops open onto the courts, while apartments and offices look down from the upper stories. *(Figures 51, 52)*

If there is a fault with the project, it is in the failure to relate the courts to Ottawa's streets. As a result, the spaces are not as heavily used or as dynamic as they might be. The courts are often entered via unmarked passages and the areas themselves are isolated not only from the streets but also from each other. They seem more like well-cared-for private spaces than like extensions of the public realm. *(Figure 53)*

The Tin House Court exemplifies this problem. This court takes its name from an elaborate house facade, made partially out of tin, which was salvaged before the rest of the house was demolished, and later hung on one of the interior court walls as "art." It is a small gesture, probably meant as a metaphor for preservation. However, it imparts an unreal character to the court, pointing out the especially fragile and delicate nature of these nineteenth-century blocks, turned partially but not entirely inside out. *(Figure 54)*

Figures 51, 52. Sussex Drive Redevelopment project, Ottawa. Views into the courts. Arthur Capling, Chief Architect.

Figure 53. Access to courts is via mid-block passages.

Figure 54. The Tin House Court.

Harbourfront, Toronto

The financially and physically modest Ottawa redevelopment stands in sharp contrast to the Toronto Harbourfront project initiated a decade later in 1972. Once again, the federal government provided the initial investment but, where the Ottawa project entailed the purchase of but four blocks, Harbourfront began with the purchase of approximately thirty-seven hectares (ninety-one acres) of land and water lots, a major chunk of Toronto's downtown waterfront.

Only days before a federal election that was expected to be, and was, extremely close, the majority Liberal government promised the City of Toronto a gift in the form of a ''waterfront park.'' While the government failed to explain what sort of park it thought might be made of an area most Torontonians thought of as an industrial wasteland, it did make it clear that the land was being made available for the benefit of the

public, and to prevent it from being swallowed up by haphazard private development.

Created from landfill during World War I, the narrow waterfront site with its five major quays, or wharves, runs along Toronto's inner harbour for just under two kilometres (one mile). As of 1972, the site contained a large number of early twentieth-century warehouses of various sizes, two mammoth grain processing and storage facilities, various commercial buildings and the Harbour Police Headquarters. The entire site was in a delapidated condition, due to construction of the elevated Gardiner Expressway (started in 1955, completed in 1966), which separated the waterfront from the city, and to the fact that much of the city's port had moved eastward to new container facilities in years previous. *(Figure 55)*

Figure 55. Harbourfront, Toronto, Site plan, the existing buildings, 1972.

Figure 56. York Quay Centre, Harbourfront, Toronto, with its outdoor cafe over the water.

Figure 57. A passage along the water's edge.

The period from 1972 to 1980 has been marked by a steady but gentle upgrading of the site, so as to make it more attractive and accessible to the public. This was done, primarily, by introducing community events and park-like elements into what quite purposefully remained an intriguing, semi-industrial waterfront landscape.

Among the most important park-like elements introduced was Harbourfront Passage, a paved route through and around the area, mostly along the water's edge, marked by planters, benches, flags, and information kiosks at important points. On the York Quay, the Direct Winters Building (formerly the warehouse and offices of a trucking company) was cleaned-up and renovated to include a theatre, an art gallery, a string of artist's studios adjacent to but set down from an interior public walkway, and a café leading onto an outdoor deck overlooking Lake Ontario. Across the street, another warehouse provides a home for a Sunday flea market during the winter months. Until recently, in warmer months, the market moved out and under the brightly-painted steel skeleton of a foundry building, erected in 1917 for the purpose of building freighters as part of the War effort. *(Figures 56, 57, 58)*

During this period of gradual change, Harbourfront has gained steadily in popularity, drawing 15,000 visitors in 1974, and 1.5 million in 1980. The future of Harbourfront, however, lies not only in the increasing number of visitors expected, but in the number of *residents* who, it is hoped by those involved, will make the area their home in the years ahead.

Figure 58. Harbourfront, the steel skeleton which formerly housed the Sunday flea market in summer months has now been demolished.

This fundamental shift in planning philosophy was proposed as part of the larger "Harbourfront Development Framework," prepared by the firm of Coombes Kirkland Berridge, for the Harbourfront Corporation in 1978. In contrast to the gentle upgrading of the site which preceeded it, this "guide to the physical future of the site" proposes a major development, entailing demolition, renovation and new construction, to create an overall system of parks, streets, services and buildings. Ambitiously hoping to attract $200 million in private investment to the site, and with a time frame of seven years for implementation (1981-1987), the proposal was approved in June 1980. At that time the owner of the site, the federal government, committed $27.5 million to help build the required infrastructure of roads, sewers and services. *(Figure 59)*

The need for such large-scale development along the water's edge was questioned by a number of people who wondered how the federal government could approve over 750,000 square metres (approximately eight million square feet) of new construction for an area originally scheduled to become a park. John Clarry, Chairman of the Metro Board of Trade's Harbourfront Committee, was among those who spoke out publicly against the development. He argued that its scale was inappropriate, and that the number of residents proposed for the area (10,000) was *at least* 5,000 too many. "People don't appreciate the kind and size of development that is being planned," he said. "This is supposed to be a parkland for the people of Metro [Toronto] . . . ."

The *Globe and Mail*, in a May 19, 1980 editorial entitled "Parkland Invaders," criticized the Harbourfront Corporation and Toronto City Hall for proposing to "push the public back behind private and public housing and commercial buildings."

Much of this concern is justified. Inevitably, views of the water from Queen's Quay will be blocked by the new construction. In an attempt to connect one end of the site with the other, a new road will be introduced along the length of the site which will bridge, divide and inexorably alter two of the existing "slips," or inlets between the quays. The largest single occupant of the site, Maple Leaf Mills Ltd., which spans two separate quays which are generally termed one, is being eliminated entirely, despite the fact that its grain elevators on the site were listed by the Toronto Historical Board for "architectural," "historical," and "contextual"

KEY
1 Harbourfront Warehouse
2 Ice & Power Houses
3 York Quay Centre
4 Pier 4
5 417 Queen's Quay
6 Le Centre Francophone
7 Produce Building
8 Channel 47
9 Canada Malting

THE RAILWAY LANDS

Proposed extension of
Queen's Quay West

Proposed
bridges

Proposed Parks at
heads of slips

Existing York Quay
Park & Pond

Proposed
pier

Proposed Spadina
Marina & Park

Existing 'Amsterdam'
pedestrian bridge

TORONTO HARBOUR

Proposed
Bathurst Park

WESTERN GAP

BATHURST QUAY | SPADINA QUAY | MAPLE LEAF QUAYS | JOHN QUAY | YORK QUAY

Figure 59. Harbourfront Development Framework, 1978 plan, Toronto. Coombes Kirkland Berridge, Urban Design.

reasons. The steel skeleton of the former foundry building on the Spadina Quay, previously the home of the Sunday flea market during warmer months, has now been demolished.

On the other hand, many of the best of the existing waterfront buildings will be retained and revitalized in the new development. The eight-storey Terminal Warehouse, a great 90,000-square-metre (approximately million-square-foot) hulk of a building which was one of Canada's early poured-in-place concrete structures, is being renovated by the Zeidler Roberts Partnership. When completed it will contain a mix of retail activities situated on the ground floors around a number of atria, a 450-seat dance auditorium on the third floor, offices in the middle levels and penthouse condominiums built on the roof.

The York Quay Centre will remain, along with a number of other buildings of architectural and historical interest, such as Le Centre Francophone and the Produce Building. Canada Malting, the area's second largest occupant, will continue its operations on Bathurst Quay at the western edge of the site. Its grain elevator, also listed by the Toronto Historical Board, will remain as well. *(Figures 60, 61)*

The proposed buildings will be arranged so as to create public courtyards and passages between them, maximizing views and actual access to the water's edge. However, in order to keep as much of the land as possible accessible to the public, three-storey housing units have been ruled out in favour of apartment buildings six-storeys and up.

The federal government's original concept of the "waterfront park," has never really been defined (or designed), and thus has always been too vague to garner much support. The Harbourfront Corporation, for instance, dismisses the "waterfront park" concept as "an idea . . . that the ninety-one acres stretching from York Street to Bathurst could simply be levelled and made into a vast green lawn."

Many of Toronto's citizens, and certainly many of its landscape architects, will always be puzzled over the suggestion that a park, must, by necessity, be a "vast green lawn." This having been said, the new "Harbourfront Development Framework" can be credited with combining an overall respect for the existing Harbourfront buildings, with a desire to use old and new buildings together to create and define a series of public spaces and promenades along the water's edge.

The firm of Coombes Kirkland Berridge has attempted to make the development as "un-project-like" as possible. Roads — in architect Michael Kirkland's words, "the virtual stuff of public space" — have been made smaller in size but more numerous. Development of all five quays will not be done at once, but in phases quay-by-quay, and probably by different architects. Whether the "sub-area," or quay-by-quay developments live up to the promise of the area in general and the Framework in particular, is something around which the historical and future character of Harbourfront will revolve.

Figures 60,61. Harbourfront, Queen's Quay Terminal. Exterior and interior renderings of the proposed renovation by Zeidler Roberts Partnership, Architects.

Granville Island, Vancouver

Three years after it had spent somewhere between $80 and $100 million on the purchase of 36.8 hectares (91 acres) of Toronto's waterfront, the federal government made a similar but smaller purchase of $11 million of leases on Granville Island, a 15.4 hectare (38-acre) industrial peninsula several minutes drive from downtown Vancouver. Unlike Harbourfront, this purchase was not part of an election campaign, but rather in response to a specially-commissioned redevelopment study done of the site, by the Vancouver firm of Thompson Berwick Pratt and Partners. The Granville Island project was also unlike Harbourfront in that the intent for the area was established at the outset.

As recommended in the study, a five-member commission was appointed to manage development of the site. Named the Granville Island Trust, the commission made the decision to retain much of the existing industry on the site prior to hiring Norman Hotson Architects to design a master plan for the "island." *(Figure 62)*

Figure 62. Granville Island, Vancouver, Master plan. Norman Hotson Architects.

Figures 63,64. Granville Island, an atmosphere of "randomness, curiosity, delight and surprise."

Architect Norman Hotson was sympathetic to the commission's goal of upgrading the existing industrial buildings and of infilling between and around these buildings so as to create facilities which would augment but not supercede the daily manufacturing of concrete and metal products on the site. "We wanted to create a public amenity," explains Hotson, "not a park. . . . In today's cities, all land uses are segregated. Our idea was to return to the original roots of settlement, to create something more village-like where all land uses are in one place."

Prefiguring Toronto's Harbourfront Development Framework of 1978, no attempt was made to separate cars and pedestrians in the 1977 Granville Island master plan. Unfortunately for cars, but perhaps fortunately for pedestrians, the existing road network on the island was, and remains, as confusing and convoluted as it could possibly be. There are still no sidewalks, permitting people to use the streets for strolling. As a result, cars crawl about the island at a speed roughly equivalent to that of the people walking alongside. *(Figures 63, 64)*

In fact, the easy-going and seemingly idiosyncratic development of the site, whereby the urban designers hoped to create an atmosphere of "randomness, curiosity, delight and surprise," imparts an air of joy. A system of plain timber posts runs along the street and through the buildings themselves, supporting colourful awnings, light fixtures and other street furnishings. The public market is housed in a warehouse renovated by the Hotson firm. Pulleys still dangle from the ceiling and a fat red pipe, supported by timber posts, snakes in and out of the building, suggesting alignment for the market stalls and lights. *(Figures 65,66,67)*

The impact of the island's simple warehouse and industrial facades has been strengthened by the judicious use of strong colour, striped awnings, and the careful placement of lighting fixtures. A number of new buildings pick up this casual theme of colourful, corrugated metal buildings with eclectic openings and fittings. New and old buildings work remarkably well with each other to impart an easy-going, accommodating and spirited character to Granville Island. *(Figures 68, 69)*

Figures 65, 66, 67. The Granville Island Public Market, interior and exterior views. Norman Hotson, Architect.

Figure 68, 69. Granville Island, The work of Barbara Dalrymple (above) and Norman Hotson (below). Simple warehouse facades, strong colours and eclectic openings and fittings are characteristic of the ''island'' as a whole.

Corridart and the 1976 Olympics, Montreal

More cerebral, much more short-lived and probably no less fun than Granville Island, Montreal's Corridart was a street festival-*cum*-urban documentary that was to have been part of the 1976 Olympics. It lasted only a week because Montreal's Mayor, Jean Drapeau, had it ripped down in the middle of the night . . . but that's getting ahead of the story.

Because it hoped that the 1976 Olympic Games would be more than just an athletic celebration, the Organizing Committee for the '76 Games (COJO) established an "Arts and Culture Programme." As part of that programme, Montreal architect Melvin Charney was hired to design, organize and coordinate his concept of an 8.4 kilometre-long (5.5 mile-long) "museum in the street."

Sherbrooke Street was the natural place for such an event. It has a long history as one of Montreal's premier boulevards, and the Olympic Park was located on its eastern end. The idea was to make Sherbrooke Street a corridor of art—"Corridart" was what Charney named it—and, according to the official Olympic book published by COJO, "a red carpet to the Olympic Park." The harmony of body and mind was to be symbolized by the display of sport and art tied together in and by one of Montreal's best-known streets.

The events leading to the construction of Olympic Park began, publically, at a press conference held by Mayor Jean Drapeau in August 1972. Obviously a great deal had transpired, privately, before the press conference. Present was the French architect, Roger Taillibert, whom Mayor Drapeau had already selected as the architect of the Olympics. Why Taillibert? Drapeau had been impressed, on a visit to Paris, with Taillibert's Parc des Prince Stadium. "I noticed," said Drapeau, "that it was something out of the ordinary, something that was later confirmed by expert engineers, who said it was something out of the ordinary."

Along with their first glimpse of the Olympic architect, the public got their first glimpse of the Olympics; Taillibert presented, in rough outline, his design. *(Figure 70)*

Unfortunately, Taillibert's Olympic buildings, along with the Olympic Village, the vast complex to house the athletes designed by Roger D'Astous and Luc Durand, would eventually present not only the 1976 Olympics, but also the City of Montreal, in a very unfavourable light. A special relationship had developed between the mayor and his chosen architect: all of Taillibert's ideas would be treated as precious artistic conceptions, their artistic integrity carefully pro-

Figure 70. 1976 Olympic Games, Montreal. Model of the Olympic Stadium and the Velodrome. Roger Taillibert, Architect.

Figure 71. Aerial view of the Olympic Stadium and the Velodrome. The Stadium tower was not completed for the games.
Roger Taillibert, Architect.

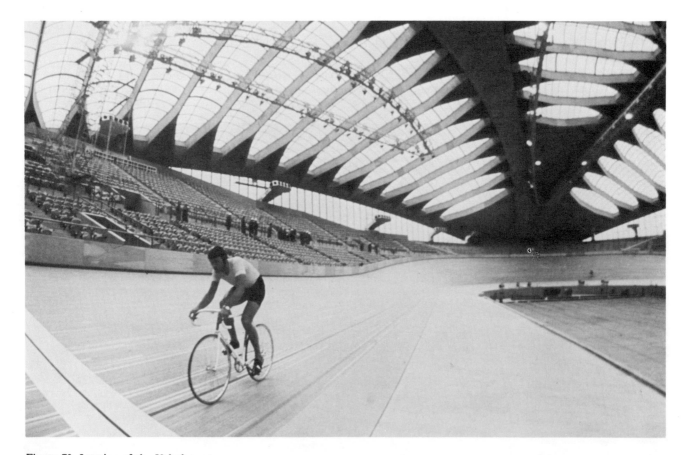

Figure 72. Interior of the Velodrome.

tected from outside interference by Mayor Drapeau himself. Costs escalated as the Quebec construction industry, when not on strike, tried to put up the huge Olympic stadium and velodrome—buildings characterized by large curving concrete planes and asymmetrical forms. The construction system was one of great complexity; each pre-cast concrete segment was, in some sense, unique and in need of special attention. The demands made of the men and materials were, at the very least, Olympian.

The velodrome, which was to house the track for Olympic cycling, came to look like "some giant Paleozoic trilobite come to rest at the bottom of the sea," in the words of architect John Hix. A concrete shell spanned 177 metres (approximately 580 feet), branching out from a single fixed support at one end to three supports on the other. The roof contained five rows of long, gently-arched skylights, making the building look from above like a prehistoric animal. From inside, the light and space are undeniably dramatic, something which is "often the case with structures which struggle with almost impossibly difficult tasks" in the words of engineer Paul Sandori who analysed the building. *(Figures 71, 72)*

No less dramatic was the Olympic stadium, seating capacity 69,000. Thirty-four concrete ribs, placed along an oval perimeter of 480 metres (1580 feet) on its long axis, formed the structure of the walls and roof of the stadium. These ribs were designed to cantilever out between 62 and 82 metres (205-269 feet) over the centre of the stadium, to define and support an oval-shaped ring which would house lighting and mechanical equipment. This oval ring would be tilted upwards towards a concrete tower which would in turn lean over the stadium to "support" a removable plastic roof for the stadium which would fit along the perimeter of the inclined oval opening. The dimensions of the tower were in keeping with the theme established elsewhere: it was to be over 170 metres (560 feet) high, and lean 53 metres (175 feet) over the stadium. *(Figures 73, 74)*

Figure 73. The Olympic Stadium under construction.

Figure 74. The Olympic Stadium during the 1976 Games.

Figure 75. The Olympic Village, built to house the athletes. Roger D'Astous and Luc Durand, Architects.

The Olympic Village to house the athletes was located across Sherbrooke Street on the south side. It bore a *striking* resemblance to the Baie des Anges residential complex on the Cote D'Azur in France, the Montreal buildings offering the same pyramidal shape and corridors on the outside which had worked so well in the south of France. *(Figure 75)*

At the time Melvin Charney was offered the contract for Corridart, "We were beginning," he says, "to suspect the *quantities* of money that were being squandered into this grandiose scheme." Indeed, even in retrospect it is difficult to comprehend the amount of money that it cost to build only *parts* of the Olympic buildings which Taillibert had originally presented in August 1972. In making his case and that of Montreal to the International Olympic Committee in 1970, Drapeau had stressed that Montreal would put on a "modest" games on a human scale, at a cost of $124 million, maximum. At the August 1972 press conference, Taillibert, in an aside to a journalist, had estimated that the Olympic stadium would cost around $60 million.

By the time the stadium was complete (but without the tower), $60 million was only enough to build two parking garages on the stadium site, although that price did include a fountain which Taillibert insisted on, at a reported cost of $8 million. Money? "Money is all Canadians and North Americans think about," said Taillibert, "money, money, money. It doesn't interest me at all. When you look at the Eiffel Tower, what remains to think about? The honorarium Eiffel received or the structure he created?"

As the costs rose for the stadium, Mayor Drapeau refused to allow the artist's conception to be changed in any way. There was shock and outrage when the final cost of the stadium was announced: $650 million. In the oft-quoted example, Seattle, Washington built a 60,000-seat domed stadium at the time of the Montreal Olympics for $60 million, the cost of those two parking garages. Alter the design? "The design is a work of art," explained Mayor Drapeau. "Never, never, never did we think of changing the design."

From an original contract of $12.3 million for the construction of the velodrome, costs escalated to $70 million. The scandal-tinged Olympic Village escalated from $30 million to $80 million before the city expropriated the buildings from the original developer /owner. From an original cost estimate of $124 million, the Olympics had escalated to an estimated $1.4 billion. And the stadium still had no roof; construction on the tower had only begun.

"The story," says Melvin Charney, recalling his involvement with the Olympics, "is unbelievable." Out of a total Olympic budget which he estimates as closer to $2 billion, he received a budget of $400,000, four months before the Olympic games were to begin, to create Corridart. "The budget was low," he says, "so I felt that, in order to stretch it the five and a half miles, I absolutely had to use the street as an exhibition of itself. Sherbrooke Street is *full* of interesting things; the idea was to highlight these things."

Figure 76. Corridart, Montreal. To anchor the scaffolding, counterweights were designed in the form of doric column bases suggesting the ruins of a "politique de grandeur." Melvin Charney, Architect.

Eleven days before the Olympics were to begin, Corridart officially opened. Conceptually, there were three "zones," although to the west and east of the central zone, Charney hoped that Sherbooke Street itself would provide the attractions, as his budget did not really enable him to enliven the street along its full length.

Thus, from Atwater to Park Avenue, to the west of the central zone, Sherbrooke Street traversed the city centre: new and old hotels; offices and clubs; the Montreal Museum of Fine Arts and Montreal's best-known art galleries. From La Fontaine Park to the Olympic Park, to the east of the central zone, was what Charney calls "the mindless strip development &whiché was allowed to take over this part of the city since the '40s — the drive-ins and instant flash that articulate a show of their own."

The central and principal zone of Corridart, the two kilometre-long part of the street between Park Avenue and La Fontaine Park, was an area of Montreal which still retained, in Charney's words, "the original sense of the place." Here are to be found the Ecole des Beaux-Arts and the Ecole d'Architecture, while the side streets were filled, in the words of the architect, "with a history of artist studios, cafés and cinemas where ideas were thrashed out and art was produced." Correspondingly, Corridart was to be most dense in this zone.

Of over four hundred entries submitted in an open competition, sixteen were selected and placed in this area. Banners hung between lamp posts created a street festival atmosphere of poetry readings, clowns and jugglers, and an outdoor café where theatre was performed.

Legende des Artistes, by Françoise Sullivan, David Moore, and Jean-Serge Champagne, was a "salute to the houses where legends are born," a series of twelve wooden boxes mounted at eye level with carefully detailed photo-montages of the artists and their environment, the immediate area of the central zone of Corridart. Using the three-dimensional volume of the boxes and a rich layering of images, the artists were able to create a series of metaphors for the richness of imagery and emotion which characterizes an urban neighbourhood.

Teletron, by Michael Haslam, consisted of a pair of old telephone booths with a neon sign flashing "teletron" overhead. Picking up one of the telephones, one could hear the tape-recorded voices both of the artists themselves and of people interviewed on the street talking about the artwork and issues of contemporary importance.

To support what he chose to call "documents," Charney rented metal scaffolding and secured it into special concrete counterweights which he had designed to look like the bases of ruined Doric columns. The "documents" (the term suggested a legal case) were mounted on the scaffolding, and came in two forms.

The first was that of photographs of people and events in the history of Sherbrooke Street. There were pictures of residents past and present along with details of their lives; "monuments," such as Mckim Mead and White's Mount Royal Club (1904-7); and important processions of the past along the street, such as the one on St. Jean Baptiste Day. There were pictures of events of every kind, from important celebrations to gruesome car accidents. *(Figure 76)*

The second sort of document consisted of a series of giant pointing hands cast out of bright red plastic. The hands were mounted on the scaffolding in such a way that they could be pivoted and pointed at the architect's discretion. Ostensibly to "guide" people through the museum, the pointing hands actually went much further. One pointed towards a typically hand-crafted, nineteenth-century wooden balcony detail, alerting the public to positive urban design features which were fast disappearing. Others, such as the one pointing to the highrise apartment building which had replaced the historic Van Horne Mansion and the one pointing at the Montreal Museum of Fine Arts, angered owners and trustees of these buildings to the point of letters and phone calls calling for the offending objects to be moved. Charney invariably complied simply by turning the hands on their pivots to point in another direction. *(Figures 77, 78)*

Charney's strongest gesture occurred on a corner lot in the central zone, a lot which had been cleared of housing for an institutional project still unbuilt by the time of the Olympics. Using the same rented scaffolding as a frame, the architect built a rough plywood, full-size facade which was the mirror image of the houses on the opposite corner. Although open to interpretation on a number of levels, this gesture was the centrepiece of Charney's exposé of municipal indifference and even destruction in Montreal. *(Figures 79, 80, 81)*

The entire Corridart exhibit had been in place for only a week, from July 6th to 13th, when Montreal's municipal workers were ordered by Drapeau's office to destroy it in the middle of the night. Why? The exhibition was a "regrettable failure," in the words of Mayor Drapeau, "an incredible pollution of Sherbrooke Street." Driving along Sherbrooke Street the Sunday before Corridart was destroyed, the Mayor described his reaction as "shocked," "humiliated" and "insulted." When the Olympics opened on July 17th, there was no trace of Corridart.

In almost every respect, the Olympic Park/Village and Corridart represented antithetical notions about architecture. Seeing architecture on the scale of the Olympics as an exclusive venue for personal impulse, Taillibert really had very little interest in Montreal, or the rest of the country for that matter. "Tomorrow's architecture," explained Taillibert, "will be acquatic."

Corridart, on the other hand, evidenced what Charney likes to call the "necessity of architecture," architecture as a kind of cultural fabric, at once the foreground of and background to community life. Accepting no limitations except those which he imposed on himself, Taillibert's designs demanded an amount of money well beyond local means.

With a minimum of money and technology, Corridart celebrated the possibility (or, again, "necessity") of public life. It pointed directly to the current dilemma

Figures 77,78. (opposite page) Corridart scaffolding on Sherbrooke Street: historical photographs and "the street as an exhibition of itself."

Figure 79. A corner of Sherbrooke Street as found: on the left, 19th century housing stock; on the right, an empty lot left by demolition.

Figure 80. The street as imagined: a photographic reconstruction.

Figure 81. Sherbrooke Street rebuilt: Charney's strongest gesture, ripped down along with the rest of Corridart on orders from the mayor. Melvin Charney, Architect.

of North American cities where, "the public content of the street," as Charney puts it, "is being removed systematically." Particularly because of the way that the municipal government responded to it, Corridart and its "documents" will be remembered both as a celebration of public life in Montreal, and as a criticism of the turn that public life in that city had taken by 1976.

IV Design, Guidelines, and the Changing Forms of Public Life

Not all the changes to public space that have occurred in Canada over the past decade have been a function of the kind of neglect and destruction implicitly criticized by Melvin Charney in his Corridart project. Nor have they been strictly the kind of reverential, piece-by-piece restoration undertaken in Ottawa's Sussex Drive courts, or the kind of wholesale salvage and recycling operations underway at Vancouver's Granville Island. Despite the publicity surrounding such projects, most recent architecture in Canadian cities has consisted of new construction. Indeed, much of this construction has been on a scale unprecedented in this country, involving immense public transportation systems and enormous tracts of privately-owned and highly-valued downtown land. In many cases, large segments of the urban fabric have been redeveloped, with only a few features or buildings selected for retention.

What has happened, however, is that the high profile of rehabilitation and infill projects has, together with the increasing scale and complexity of urban life, promoted an awareness and an appreciation of public spaces that respond to cultural practices and aspirations. While the awareness of new forms of public life has derived in part from an architectural vogue, it has in some instances resulted from city and provincial government guidelines that have been established to protect and enhance the historical, social, and urbane qualities of Canadian cities.

Ironically, the scale of much of the new development has been in large measure a result of government policies, particularly at the federal level. The post-war policies of the Central Mortgage and Housing Corporation fostered the growth of colossal international private development corporations, making Canadian-based companies like Olympia & York and Cadillac Fairview among the largest developers in North America. The massive redevelopment of which these developers are capable has called forth the complex zoning by-laws and planning guidelines that occupy increasingly the agendas of municipal councils.

The result of renewed interest in history and context, combined with such guidelines, is that developers and architects have begun mixing less lucrative uses with highly profitable ones, less efficient but historically venerable buildings with new super-efficient structures, and public areas with commercially profitable leasable space. Such projects as Calgary's Plus 15 pedestrian system, Toronto's Spadina Subway, Vancouver's Robson Square, Toronto's Eaton Centre, and Montreal's Complexe Desjardins, while expressive of technological and economic optimism, reflect different aspects of a growing awareness of the larger urban and cultural order.

Plus 15, Calgary

In urban systems like Calgary's downtown pedestrian plan and Toronto's Spadina subway line, the scale and complexity of the projects has required a generation of planning and implementation, and the involvement of scores of different interest groups, professionals, artists, and ultimately on a daily basis, millions of citizens.

Calgary has encouraged high-rise, high-density redevelopment in the downtown core. However in 1970, the city implemented a policy intended to mitigate the effects of such redevelopment. Hailed as the most comprehensive system of its kind in North America, Plus 15's main feature is a network of bridges, plazas, and climate-controlled walkways to and through buildings. The passages are raised one level (or 15 feet, hence the name, Plus 15) above ground to allow for the uninterrupted passage of traffic below. (Actually the height has been raised three feet higher, due to traffic accidents involving 15-foot high bridges and crane-carrying trucks.) *(Figure 82)*

The Plus 15 system is only possible in a city like Calgary. The amount of new high-rise construction ensures that connections can be readily accommodated in new designs, and that the developers of buildings across from one another can split the costs of providing bridges. Unlike Montreal and Toronto, cities which have routed pedestrians into climate-controlled tunnels under neighbouring towers, Calgary's high water table precluded an underground system.

The bridges have been installed in buildings within a section of downtown called the "must area." Developers of new buildings in the "must area" *must* link into the system at their own expense, or pay the city to have it done for them. Conversely, buildings outside the "must area" can earn extra floor space allowances if they provide Plus 15 bridges to adjacent buildings. The formula for the bonus has been: extra floor space = 30

Figure 82. Interior of Plus 15 bridge between Provincial Court and Remand Centre, Calgary. Jack Long and the New Street Group, Architects.

Figure 83. 1967 Plan of Pedestrian System, including mall, lanes and Plus 15 system, Calgary. Affleck, Desbarats, Dimakopoulos and Sise, Architects.

times the area of the bridge. Still undergoing redefinition, the system is now being modified to better coordinate with other systems for car and pedestrian movement, and to achieve other downtown planning aims.

Why design a separate system for pedestrians? Apart from the obvious discomfort of harsh winter weather, the City of Calgary Planning Department's 1969 "Downtown Development Guidelines" justified Plus 15 by claiming that it would "ensure adequate provision for the pedestrian . . . without infringing unduly upon the rights of the individual to obtain a fair development of his property." Thus, just as the extent to which a developer could cover and occupy his land is regulated, so too is the nature of public access to the Plus 15 realm. An "Activity Policy" determined that half the space fronting on the walkways had to be for "retail, cultural, entertainment, or amusement" uses. For an apartment building, the policy required that only a quarter of the frontage be for "activity."

The pedestrian system is not limited to the street-crossing bridges. The original plan drawn up by Affleck, Desbarats, Dimakopoulos, Lebensold and Sise in 1967 emphasized the development of former lane spaces between the backs and sides of buildings for pedestrian use as well. The second floors of buildings would be required, both by the "Activity Policy" and by the pervasiveness of the pedestrian zone, to provide a new type of semi-public space linking the bridges to other bridges and to plazas located in the middle of blocks. *(Figure 83)*

Although the Plus 15 system was conceived of as a policy of benefit primarily to pedestrians, it is essentially controlled by, and of considerable benefit to, the private sector. For one of the drawbacks of establishing a system so completely predicated on new construction is that the interests of small property owners are not addressed. Their inability to link into the system has had a detrimental effect on street-level shops and on Calgary's street life generally.

Nevertheless, Harold Hanen, a Senior Planner in Calgary's Planning Department at the time when Plus 15 was first conceived, continues to endorse the city's pedestrian policy, insisting that, "Plus 15 has had a very positive effect on architecture in Calgary. It has established the interdependence of buildings on each other, and tends to make architects less arrogant, more aware of each other's buildings."

The strengths and weaknesses of the system are amply demonstrated by the Toronto-Dominion Square's Devonian Gardens, to date the only major interior space specifically designed to fit into the Plus 15 network. The bank's black steel and glass tower sits

Figure 84. Toronto-Dominion Square, Calgary. Fronting on the 8th Avenue pedestrian mall, but above it and behind the dark, sloping glass, the Devonian Gardens. J. H. Cook Architects and Engineers, in association with Skidmore Owings and Merrill, Architects.

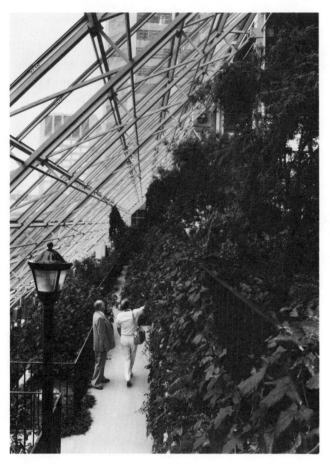

Figure 85. Interior of the Devonian Gardens, Toronto Dominion Square, Calgary.

Figure 86. The Hudson's Bay Store, street-level arcade, 8th Avenue Mall, Calgary.

atop a four-storey podium on 3rd Street S.W., between 7th Avenue and 8th Avenue. Eighth Avenue is itself a pedestrian precinct created by partial closure to automobile traffic. *(Figure 84)*

From the Plus 15 level upward, much of this podium has been devoted to an indoor garden open to the public. Landscaped terraces rise through several levels, and walkways criss-cross the mass of vegetation which has grown into a dense jungle. Warm sunshine streams through the sloped glass during even the most severe winter weather. The gardens are used by lunching office workers, and include a small playground and a space for displaying art. *(Figure 85)*

In marked contrast to the nearby Hudson's Bay store with its gracious, street-level arcades, the T-D Square satisfies the city's rules for pedestrian movement, but only insofar as the rules contribute revenue to its retail activities. The Devonian Gardens, its one real amenity, is accessible exclusively via a shopping mall, and is all but invisible from 8th Avenue below because

of the Square's relentlessly dark glass surface. *(Figure 86)*

The ability of Plus 15 to accommodate itself to a non-commercial setting is illustrated by the connections it provides between a number of government buildings located east of the commercial part of Calgary's downtown core. Here the Provincial Court and Remand Centre, designed by Jack Long and the New Street Group (1975), is connected by Plus 15 bridges to two other institutions of fairly recent construction, the Police Station and the Public Library. These latter are connected to City Hall, a pre-World War I sandstone structure, via its Administration Building Annex.

It is one thing for stores to be off the same hallway as the Devonian Gardens, but is clearly another for a remand centre/court house and police station to be sharing hallways with a public library. It is especially incongruous to walk out from the lobby of the library into the halls of a police station and to see uniformed police on their way to court. Even more disconcerting are the hallways themselves, a concatenation of concrete, bullet-proof glass, steel, aluminum, planters, and displays, separating the mid-block Plus 15 zone from the back lane where prisoners are delivered in police cars for detention and trial. *(Figure 87)*

The Court and Remand Centre's architectural adjustment to the Plus 15 is necessarily more abrupt than that of commercial buildings, like the Toronto-Dominion Square. The low-rise Court and Remand Centre building is organized visually as if the ground level were a basement and the second level were the ground level. Downstairs is the entrance to the jail; the jail's administrative offices present a blank concrete wall to cars speeding by on the one-way street. The second level contains a large lobby encircled by courtrooms. Inserted between the entry to the Remand Centre and its upper floors of dormitories and cells, the Court House generously accommodates the Plus 15 that is routed through it by providing a comfortably large atrium, with refreshingly low lighting levels and casual furniture. It is a space that seems to address the pedestrian, pausing on his walk, say, from City Hall to the Board of Education building across the street as much as it replies to the functional need for lobby space for the courts. *(Figures 88, 89)*

Figure 87. View of the Provincial Court and Remand Centre from across the street, Calgary. Jack Long and the New Street Group, Architects.

Figure 88. Provincial Court and Remand Centre, interior view of the Courthouse atrium, Calgary. The atrium is connected with the Plus 15 system.

Figure 89. Front of Provincial Court and Remand Centre, viewed from Plus 15 across the street, Calgary.

While Calgary's Plus 15 may represent an improvement on Toronto and Montreal's subterranean concourses and Edmonton's "Pedway" (a little-implemented system which is randomly above, below, and at ground level), it suffers from a lack of ingenuity. Traditionally, a separation between pedestrians and vehicular traffic has been motivated by the double aims of increasing the efficiency of the roadway, and creating an idyllic promenade, far removed from the exhaust fumes. Although it is generally agreed that vehicular efficiency is best served by a grid pattern of streets, there is no reason for pedestrians to be similarly regimented. Despite providing a respite from car traffic, the Plus 15 system is as rigidly gridded as the abandoned sidewalks below, and has not fulfilled its original promise of providing pedestrian oases in the middle of blocks.

Figure 90. A drawing from New York's visionary twenties: "General view of a city square showing the additional possibility of a second level of pedestrian traffic at the height of a ten-storey setback." Harvey Wiley Corbett, Architect.

Figure 91. "Preliminary Town Planning Scheme — General Plan," 1914, Calgary. Thomas Mawson, town planner.

Town planner Thomas Mawson, whose 1914 plan for Calgary envisioned an ideal garden-city, would recognize few of his dreams for winding, treed promenades in the Plus 15 bridges. The Plus 15 realm is too often an impoverished version of a well-regulated public sidewalk system, and the bridges have too often fostered an unwarranted degree of control of collective space by private interests. *(Figures 90, 91)*

Spadina Subway, Toronto

Toronto, too, had planned for the common good in anticipation of future growth. As early as 1909, a subway system was proposed. The Bloor Street Viaduct was designed to carry subway trains, as well as cars and horse-drawn carriages, across the Don Valley. The Yonge Street Subway line, Canada's first, opened in 1954.

Not long after the Yonge line was in operation, the city's Metropolitan Planning Board, in anticipation of even greater growth, proposed that the Spadina Subway line be built in conjunction with a new expressway. The idea at the time was first to install the largely above-ground line as a sort of commuter rail line, and later to build the north and southbound expressway lanes on either side. However, over twenty years were to pass before the opening of the Spadina line's eight stations in 1978. The delay was due in part to virulent citizen opposition to the expressway, and to the destruction of neighbourhoods and homes.

In 1963 work began on the northern terminus of the expressway at Highway 401. By 1966, the Spadina Expressway, was finished from Wilson to Lawrence. Approximately half of the eight hundred houses slated for demolition had been torn down.

As the expressway approached the older, more densely settled areas to the south, citizen protest reached a crescendo. Many shared Marshall McLuhan's view that the high-speed route, slicing through established neighbourhoods, would be "a cement kimono for Toronto." The subway was to be the silk lining, but few were won over by its appeal.

Public hearings began in 1970 with the result that the Provincial Government stepped in to stop the expressway. "If we are building a transportation system to serve the automobile," Premier William Davis declared to the legislature in 1971, "the Spadina Expressway would be a good place to start. But if we are building a transportation system to serve people, the Spadina Expressway is a good place to stop." For the next four years, attention shifted from the completed-but-unopened portion of the expressway between Wilson and Lawrence avenues to the excavated-but-unbuilt portion south from Lawrence to Eglinton Avenue, the infamous "Spadina ditch." In the context of the 1971 campaign, which Premier Davis won in part because of his promise to stop the expressway, U.S. architect Buckminster Fuller proposed a linear village of housing and stores to be built in the ditch. "Project Spadina," as the Fuller scheme was called, was designed to fill the sides of the ditch with terraced, low-rise

Figure 92. Map of Toronto showing stations on the Spadina subway line, Spadina Expressway indicated by heavy line. Toronto Transit Commission Staff, under the direction and approval of the Commissioners.

buildings, thereby inverting what Fuller characterized as "the glass cliffs of the usual high-rises."

Like many campaign promises, Project Spadina was quickly forgotten, leaving Metro Council, the municipal body governing Toronto and its suburbs, to take charge. Metro Council, which has traditionally favoured suburban interests, wanted to pave the ditch, open it as an "arterial road," and run the Spadina Subway right down its median strip. By then, however, the Spadina alignment, although precisely the one recommended in 1956, was only one of twenty alternative subway routes being considered. After further study, Metro's Executive Committee voted to change the subway alignment to Bathurst Street where the city's ravines would be less disturbed, fewer houses would be destroyed, and the subway would run through areas of greater population density. *(Figure 92)*

In considering alternative routes, the City was confronted with the issue which had plagued the subway/ expressway from the start: an expressway is ideally situated on the suburban fringe, while a subway works best in the heart of the urban fabric. Despite this central point, Metro Council chose in 1972, as a final "compromise," to construct the Spadina Subway down the abandoned ditch.

Subway construction had been advancing along the centre of the ditch for five months when, in January 1975, the Davis government agreed to pave it. The paving was made palatable by the condition that from Lawrence to Eglinton avenues, the Spadina Expressway would be called an "arterial road with limited access." Since arterial roads, like Yonge Street, are merely wide city streets that do not have limited access, the semantic sleight-of-hand was widely recognized for the contradiction it was.

Nonetheless, on September 7, 1976, travelling along the freshly-paved road for the first time, drivers found that south of Lawrence, the William R. Allen Expressway was duly marked as the "William R. Allen Arterial Road." And because this road dead ends abruptly at a traffic light on Eglinton Avenue West, drivers waiting in the long rush-hour line-ups had ample time to contemplate the Spadina line's new, air-conditioned trains travelling up and down the median strip.

In response to criticism of the sterility of Toronto's earlier engineer-designed stations, the Toronto Transit Commission (T.T.C.) decided to involve not only architects but local artists in the design of the Spadina stations. Kendal and Glencairn were allotted to Adamson Associates, Dupont and Lawrence to Dunlop Farrow Aitken (DFA), and Eglinton and Yorkdale to Arthur Erickson Associates. The T.T.C. meanwhile reserved the right to design what it considered the two most "difficult" stations, their difficulty being deemed a function of technical rather than architectural or urban design parameters. An independent art consultant, Nina Wright, was retained to conduct a feasibility study on the choice of art for the stations.

By the time the stations were to be designed, demolition of historic buildings had become sufficiently unpopular that Adamson Associates devoted considerable effort to preserving the turn-of-the-century Romanesque Revival house that stood on the site of the

Figure 93. Construction of Spadina Subway Station, at Kendal Avenue, Toronto. Moving the house on steel rails. Adamson Associates, Architects.

southern-most station. The house was placed on steel beams and rolled aside while the underground station was constructed. Afterwards, like an elaborate stage set, the partially-gutted house was rolled back into place and refurbished to serve as the flagship Spadina Station. The former front lawn was replaced by a brick patio, and the house now sits several inches below its original level. Although these changes were the source of some criticism from architectural historians who felt that the house's relationship to the ground should have been more accurately maintained, the resulting streetscape looked much as it had previously, putting to rest fears that the new subway line would disrupt the character of Spadina Road. Appropriately, the art installed at the Spadina Station is a Joyce Wieland quilt, "Barren Ground Caribou," a work of similarly gentle preservationist leanings. *(Figures 93, 94)*

Stations at Dupont and at Lawrence (both by Dunlop Farrow Aitken) make their presence felt at street level, but as at Spadina, they do so in ways appropriate to their context. At Dupont, the presence of the underground subway stop is emphatically announced above ground by its entrances: two arresting, transparent pavilions framed with bright orange metal straps and placed on diagonally opposite corners. In an area where housing, shops, and light industry are mixed with few common architectural qualities, the two identically-formed pavilions help to define the intersection. *(Figure 95)*

At Lawrence, as at the other stations along the median strip, the design challenge was to create a sense of place within a landscape in perpetual motion. The use of the Spadina median, with its long history of conflict, as a site for public architecture, seemed to demand

Figure 94. Completed Spadina Station, with house back in place. Adamson Associates, Architects.

Figure 95. Exterior of Dupont Subway Station, Spadina Line, Toronto. Dunlop Farrow Aitken, Architects.

Figure 96. Exterior of Lawrence Subway Station showing bus platforms, Spadina Line, Toronto. Dunlop Farrow Aitken, Architects.

Figure 97. Interior of Lawrence Station, subway platform.

extraordinary gestures. DFA again used bright orange pavilions on either side of the street with spectacular effect. In this case, however, the pavilions are not identical. From the larger one, on the south side of Lawrence, "Spacing . . . Aerial Highways," a vibrantly-coloured tile mural by Claude Breeze, extends out and over the Allen Expressway as it passes under Lawrence Avenue. Like the mural, the placement of the station's bus platforms out over the expressway takes advantage of the dramatic potential offered by the intersection of different modes of transportation. *(Figures 96, 97, 98)*

Figure 98. Exterior of Lawrence Station, showing Claude Breeze mural.

Figure 99. Yorkdale Station, Toronto, Exterior. Arthur Erickson Associates, Architects.

The most extraordinary of all the stations along the median is the Yorkdale Station, designed by Arthur Erickson Associates. Yorkdale is the slickest transit station of any kind in Canada, with a unique location adjacent to a shopping plaza. Architecturally, it relates only to the median strip and to the subway trains that drive along it, not to the shopping centre and commuter parking lots it serves. *(Figure 99)*

Shoppers arriving by transit have to cross a vast, windy, shopping centre parking lot to get from the station to the mall, a situation which might have been mitigated had Hans Blumenfeld, a planner involved with the Spadina line, prevailed over the plaza owners' attitude towards public transportation:

> I got the T.T.C. and Yorkdale people (Trizec Equities) together, and I tried to get the shopping centre people to put a direct entrance (from the subway station) into their shopping centre. But they were adamant. They said, "No, we already have all our leases, and our experience is that only 7% of our people come by public transit.

In other negotiations with the City regarding parking space for commuters from neighbouring areas, Trizec offered space — over half a kilometre from the station. As if anticipating the plaza's indifference to it, the Yorkdale Station is, except for an unavoidable pedestrian bridge extended out over the expressway to the plaza's parking lot, coolly detached from the plaza. *(Figure 100)*

Modelled after the subway trains, the silvery stainless steel-covered platform glamorizes the industrial image of the subway, making it seem as urbane and sophisticated to ride the T.T.C. as to shop in the elegant steel and glass boutiques downtown on Bloor Street. Trains emerging from the Yorkdale stop, with its curved steel cladding and subway car-like windows, appear to glide as naturally as snakes gliding out of a former skin.

Figures 101,102. Yorkdale Station, Toronto. Interior.

Figure 100. Yorkdale Station, Toronto. Aerial view showing bridge to Yorkdale shopping plaza in foreground, right.

From the perspective of motorists driving by, the icy and sleek Yorkdale Station monumentalizes the passage of trains through it.

Yorkdale Station's platform is, like the Lawrence Station mural, an instance where the architects' and the artists' work are closely synchronized. Delicate steel ribs support a vaulted glass roof which wraps down over the north and south ends of the platform, allowing views out over the train tracks beyond. The steel ribs hold a neon sculpture by Michael Hayden composed of hoops of colours of the spectrum, which are illuminated sequentially, triggered by the arrival of trains. The illumination is best appreciated when the sky is dark. Hayden's "Arc en Ciel," a mechanical rainbow of lights "travelling" against the glass of the ceiling, serves as an analogue to the movement of trains through the space and alludes to the sky overhead. *(Figures 101, 102, 103)*

Figure 103. Yorkdale Station, Toronto, Roof showing Michael Hayden's neon sculpture, "Arc en Ciel." Arthur Erickson Associates, Architects.

In its idealized expression of subway travel, the Yorkdale Station clearly raises problems that remain unresolved about the Spadina system as a whole. The station's ability to stand on its own architecturally, dependent only on the trains' operation, is a reminder of the line's isolation from the established settlement that is ordinarily its lifeblood. In contrast to the subway systems of Vienna and Paris, where engineers, artists, and architects have collaborated to design systems that serve as models of urban design, the Spadina line bears witness to the consequences of politicians, planners, developers and architects independently pursuing their respective concerns.

Robson Square and Provincial Law Courts, Vancouver

Vancouver's Robson Square and Provincial Law Courts, Toronto's Eaton Centre and Commerce Court, and Montreal's Complexe Desjardins demonstrate both positive and negative aspects of urban renewal. These recent large-scale developments have provided the central areas of these cities with new types of semi-public and public space. In accommodating the interests of large and complex clients, the designers of these megadevelopments have attempted, with varying degrees of success, to balance economies of scale with vibrant images of social life.

Robson Square and the Provincial Law Courts (Arthur Erickson Associates, 1980) form a new government and civic centre for Vancouver, occupying three blocks of prime downtown real estate owned by the B.C. government. Running from north to south, Blocks 51/61/71, as they were referred to prior to the new construction, became notorious for the debate that raged over whether the land should be used for a 55-storey tower, or a public park or square. *(Figure 104)*

The new Law Courts have also replaced courts previously housed in the Neo-classical building at the northern end of Block 51 with an all-new complex on Block 71. The former Court House is being restored and has been designated for use by the Vancouver Art Gallery. Named in honour of a nineteenth-century premier of British Columbia, John Robson, the development is long and narrow and bracketed on both ends by law court buildings, the one a fine example of nineteenth-century architect Francis Rattenbury's work, the other representative of the recent architecture of Arthur Erickson Associates. Together, the two buildings invite comparison of architectural styles and social attitudes as they have evolved over the past century. *(Figure 105)*

The portion of Block 51 south of the Rattenbury Court House has been carved out to create Robson Square. Lined on its east and west edges by restaurants and food concessions, the Square extends southward under Robson Street to the mid-point of Block 61. From there, a low-rise B.C. government office building extends still further southward, spanning Smithe Street, and ending just as it reaches Block 71. Block 71 is blanketed by the new Law Courts building, an eight-storey edifice characterized by its stepped concrete frame structure. Arthur Erickson's predilection for creating buildings as landscape, seen earlier in his proposal for the National Gallery competition, has found its largest-scale realization to date in Robson Square. In

Figure 104. Robson Square and the Law Courts, Vancouver, Site plan, Blocks 51/61/71. Arthur Erickson Associates, Architects.

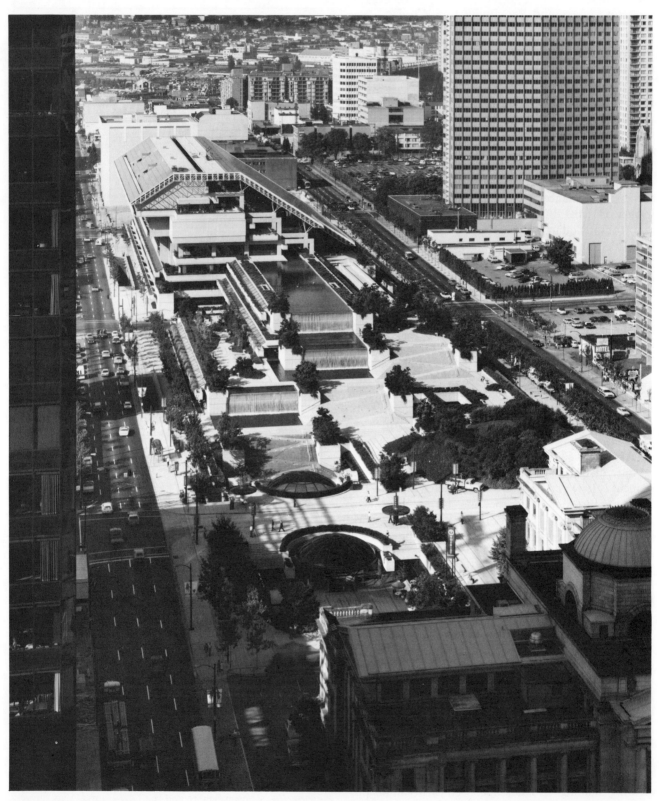

Figure 105. Robson Square and the Law Courts, Vancouver,
Aerial view. Arthur Erickson Associates, Architects.

Figure 106. Robson Square, Vancouver, View looking north.

a few more years, the concrete walls of the government office building will have all but disappeared behind the vast plantings along its terraces. *(Figure 106)*

The size and southward bias of Robson Square's park and paths provide a dramatic forecourt to the Law Courts. A sophisticated series of visual and sensual cues draws the visitor through the complex. "Stramps," a hybrid stair/ramp suggestive of the ceremonial architecture of ancient civilizations, make what are, in actuality, extreme level changes seem enticing. Thousands of plants and two spectacularly-engineered waterfalls address the approaching pedestrian, compelling him

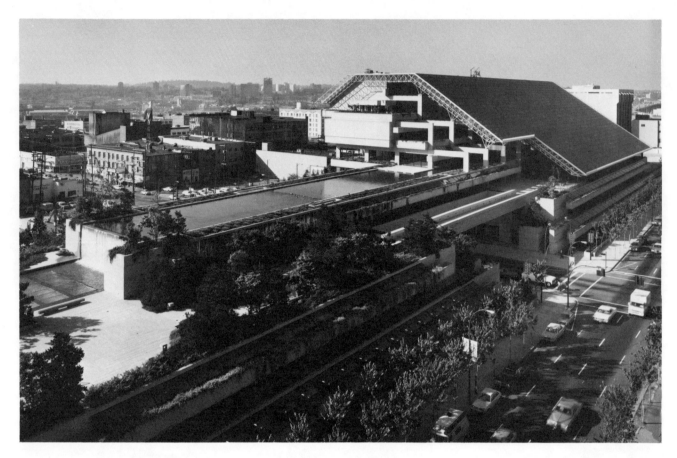

Figure 107. Government Office Complex, Smithe Street overpass, and the Law Courts, Vancouver. Arthur Erickson Associates, Architects.

along for three blocks through a man-made landscape with much of the interest and complexity of the natural environment. *(Figure 107)*

The natural-seeming flow of space ends abruptly at Nelson Street. A short stair descends to an ordinary city sidewalk where the concrete end-wall of a very ordinary building is all that one can see. Despite the tantalizing suggestion that this masterfully-contoured landscape is a continuous or, even better, a typical piece of downtown Vancouver, it is in fact all too finite and unique, terminated on both ends by buildings which are raised significantly above street level. *(Figure 108)*

Like all modern inventions, the project challenges preconceptions of the ways things have been or ought to be. The two end buildings now face each other across Robson Square, rather than the streets on which they sit. The definition of city blocks and streets has been overruled by pedestrian passages that have been made above and below ground level.

The glass-roof lobby of the Law Courts where, by

Arthur Erickson's own description, "Justice must not only be done but be seen to be done," is a huge, theatrical space. The flat public passageway is in notable contrast to the terraces of court rooms, and the concealed corridors beyond which judges and the accused travel, segregated for security purposes. There is nothing for the casual visitor to do in the lobby but to marvel at the scale of the space. Similarly, the public space of Robson Square, severed from casual sidewalk access by its complex arrangement of levels, suggests ancient Roman fora or Greek amphitheatres, and appears to be intended for occasions of extreme formality. *(Figure 109)*

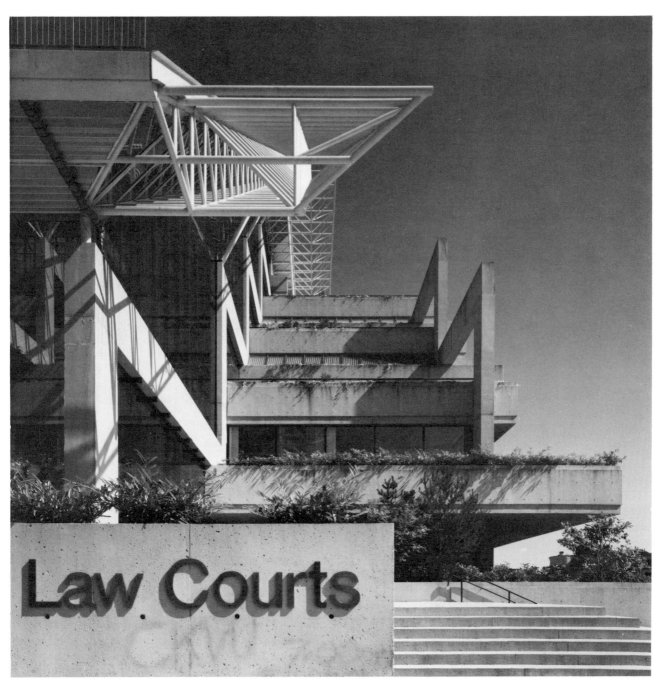

Figure 108. Law Courts, Vancouver, corner of Nelson and Howe Streets.

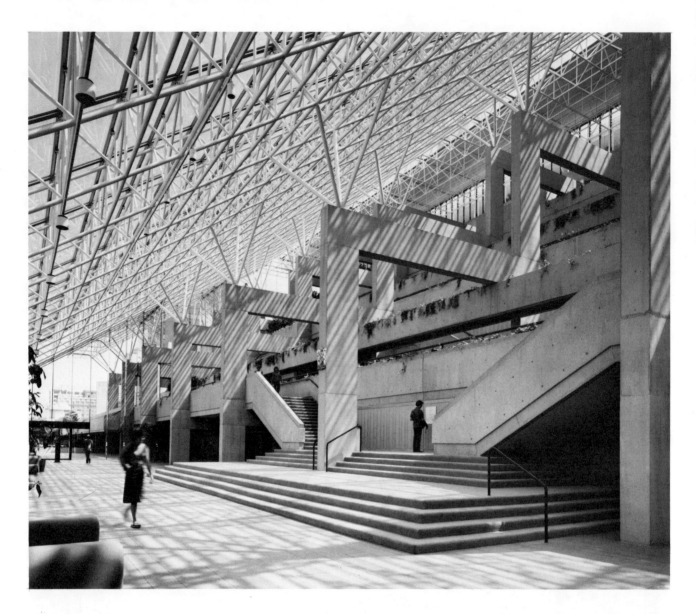

Figure 109. Law Courts, Vancouver, Interior, Public Lobby. Arthur Erickson Associates, Architects.

Robson Square offers an image of the City as a place of serene but austere beauty. No discordant elements, no jarring electric signs, no traffic, no mullions to interrupt the glassy expanse of the Law Courts' roof. It holds up an ascetic standard to what Arthur Erickson has called "our trash-oriented society." He comments that, "Our surroundings, most of our food, what we read, what we see in films, hear in music, desensitizes our perceptions. We learn an indifference to things rather than a respect and love of our surroundings."

By imposing this ascetic standard on the surrounding area rather than accepting cues from it, the architecture attempts to dictate exactly what our perceptions of it should be.

Eaton Centre, Toronto

Toronto's Eaton Centre (Bregman & Hamann and Zeidler Partnership, 1981) also engulfs its site, and in so doing, sets the tone for the surrounding area. Like most North American shopping malls, Eaton Centre does not itself have a centre. It consists of a new Eaton store which anchors the development on its northern end, two high-rise office towers, and the 274-metre-long (900 foot) glass-roofed Galleria. Flanked on both sides by three levels of stores, the Galleria links the flagship Eaton store to the century-old Simpson's store which, although not part of the development, effectively serves as the project's southern boundary. *(Figure 110)* A final phase of the development will include an office complex for Bell Canada (Parkin Partnership, 1982) and, eventually, residential buildings.

The development already covers what were five city blocks. Two former cross-streets have been closed, their original locations marked among four major entrances to the complex at Dundas Street, Trinity Mall, Albert, and Queen streets. Seen from Yonge Street, the entrances help to divide the massive project visually; inside, they widen to facilitate connections between street and underground levels. *(Figures 111, 112)*

Unlike Robson Square, the Eaton Centre's exterior does not create a narrative sequence. Instead of rising from a beginning to a climax with episodes along the way, it is consistently eventful and diversified throughout its considerable length. The two towers are similar in detail, but their slightly offset positions at opposite ends of the Galleria respond to the landmarks and streets that make up their immediate context. Along Yonge Street, the porcelain-enamelled skin of the new Eaton store (E.L. Hankinson with associate architects Parkin Millar & Associates; Bregman & Hamann as consulting architects and structural engineers) folds in and out around its columns, distinguishing it from the grey and white cladding of the rest of the Centre, while emphasizing its similarly massive scale.

The Centre's various entrances and shop-front details, also framed prominently with structural members, impart an image of controlled diversity. Along the western, rear wall of the Eaton Centre, which will eventually be hidden behind the final developments of the master plan, a frankly industrial use of materials reveals a rationally organized megastructure. The individuality of commercial outlets is therefore only perceived along Yonge Street. *(Figure 113)*

Figure 110. Site Plan of Eaton Centre, Toronto. Bregman & Hamann and the Zeidler Partnership, Architects.

Figure 111. Dundas Street entry to the Eaton Centre, inside the glass entrance canopy, looking up from the first level below grade. Bregman & Hamann and the Zeidler Partnership, Architects.

The historic Trinity Church, formerly set off on a small square, is now largely surrounded by the back of the Eaton store, its parking garage, and the northern half of the Galleria. The Salvation Army Building (John B. Parkin Associates, 1956) to the south on Albert Street, another local landmark, appears similarly absorbed by the development. The treatment of these buildings is indicative of the problems architects encounter introducing a bland suburban building form (a shopping centre) into a highly differentiated urban site. While the historic buildings are regarded as necessary souvenirs of a more individualized era, the application of current formulas for economic efficiency to construction tends to generalize the context in which those souvenirs are now set. *(Figure 114)*

Figure 112. Eaton Centre. Entrance to the Galleria, south of the Eaton's store and on a cross axis with Trinity Square.

Figure 113. View of Eaton Centre from Bay Street, the "back" side, just south of Trinity Church.

Figure 114. A model of the Eaton Centre complex photo-collaged onto an aerial view of the site, Toronto. Bregman & Hamann and the Zeidler Partnership Architects.

What distinguishes the Eaton Centre from so many other large-scale downtown commercial developments is the linking space of the Galleria mall. Its uppermost level, which contains the most expensive range of stores, has been detailed with awnings and trees planted flush with the floor to resemble a street. As in preservation projects discussed in the previous chapter, the top-lit passage of the Galleria gives new value to mid-block space, and makes it habitable year-round. Within the limits of commercial mega-development, the Eaton Centre Galleria creates a sense of place both on the scale of the individual, with benches and gardening, and on the city scale, with connections to subways, and to a lesser extent, streets. *(Figures 115, 116)*

Figure 115. Eaton Centre. Inside the Galleria, looking south to the Queen Street entrance.

Figure 116. The Yonge Street facade of the Eaton Centre, showing the use of stair towers, steel structure, balconies, benches and lights to create a scale appropriate to the pedestrian life of Yonge Street. Bregman & Hamann and the Zeidler Partnership, Architects.

By consolidating six hectares (fifteen acres) of downtown land into a single parcel, the Eaton Centre's consortium client (Cadillac Fairview Corporation, the T. Eaton Company Ltd., and the Toronto-Dominion Bank) has indeed gentrified a formerly sleazy strip of Yonge Street. But the design elements that make the Centre a hospitable rather than a hostile presence on Yonge Street were effected partly through the political pressures exerted on the developer by municipal politicians. At their urging and in exchange for permitting street closures, the Centre provides such positive urban design features as shopfronts on Yonge, access at the former street locations, and concealment of the parking garage that fronts onto Yonge Street. The success of the Centre as an urban place bears testimony to the importance of making civic as well as commercial priorities articulate.

Place Desjardins, Montreal

Like the Eaton Centre consortium, the backers of the Complexe Desjardins selected a derelict site in Montreal's downtown core for a development to combine high-rise office space with a variety of commercial facilities.

The developer of Complexe Desjardins is the Desjardins Cooperative Movement, a group of Quebec credit unions *(caisses populaires)* and affiliated trust and insurance companies together with the then-Liberal provincial government. Although the venture was ostensibly independent of party politics, it pointedly symbolized the ascendance of French-Canadian initiative in the Quebec economy. As Claude Ryan pointed out in a 1976 *Le Devoir* editorial, the pressure on the developer to succeed was made greater by the fact that the *caisses populaires'* financial growth was founded on the savings of *"les petits gens."*

The Desjardins group used the prominence of its 3.2 hectare (eight-acre) site to promote the venture. By assembling and rebuilding on all properties from Ste. Catherine south to Dorchester Boulevard and between Jeanne-Mance and Saint-Urbain streets, the developers promised they would create "the concrete symbol of a fierce determination to remodel the city, and thereby, the man on the street."

The replacement of the tightly-packed, low-rise brick buildings with the huge new concrete Complexe was to be the architectural analogue of the transformation of Québecois society by the *Révolution Tranquille*.

The site was aligned, on a north-south axis, with the historic Place d'Armes in Old Montreal, and the Place des Arts complex of theatres (Affleck, Desbarats, Dimakopoulos, Lebensold, Michaud and Sise, 1963), both of which are subway stops. The Complexe Desjardins in fact has access to the Place des Arts station via a tunnel under Ste. Catherine. *(Figures 117, 118)*

The Complexe Desjardins consists of two principal parts. The first is the Complexe, which is made up of four high-rise buildings set on a continuous three-storey podium, or *basilaire*. The podium takes the place of the former low-rise commercial buildings, all traces of which were removed.

Figure 117. Aerial view of Complexe Desjardins, Montreal. La Société la Haye-Ouellet, urban design.

Figure 118. Exterior of Complexe Desjardins, viewed from Place des Arts, Montreal.

The second part is Place Desjardins, a covered, climate-controlled .4 hectare (one acre) area in the centre of the podium. Surrounded by shops, bank branches and restaurants, Place Desjardins is an open space of roughly the same size as Place d'Armes. It is one storey below street level, but is connected by escalators to a street-level Promenade that runs through the middle of the Complexe from north to south. *(Figure 119)*

As an indication of its fierce determination to make Place Desjardins work, the management established an Animation Service to work full-time co-ordinating activities. Groups can schedule displays on such diverse subjects as art, astronomy, or the environment. Tapings for live radio and TV shows are a regular feature. The monthly spectacular, *"Les Vendredis de la pleine lune,"* is one of the Animation Service's most popular activities, featuring live performances by Québecois singers and entertainers. Unlike Eaton Centre, Place Desjardins has Muzak, coloured floodlights, and other accoutrements typical of suburban shopping plazas. It has been defended by local architects and critics as an expression of anti-elitist cultural aspirations. *(Figures 120, 121)*

The Complexe is much harder to like than the Place. Its four pre-cast concrete towers (three for offices, one for the Méridien Hotel) rise out of the podium near, but not at, the four corners of the block. They are not artfully aligned, like Mies van der Rohe's Westmount Square in the heart of Montreal's wealthiest English-speaking residential district, to suggest different sculptured compositions when viewed from afar. Nor are they consolidated into a single, recognizable emblem like I. M. Pei's cruciform Place Ville Marie, several blocks away at the nerve centre of the anglo business district. The Complexe's architects grouped the four towers clockwise in order of height. The shortest, the hotel, is across from the grassy corner of Place des Arts; the tallest two, at thirty-two and forty-one storeys respectively, face the traffic of Dorchester Boulevard. This pinwheel arrangement of the towers reinforces the existing segregation of pedestrian and vehicular traffic: the buildings are lowest across from the park where there are the greatest number of pedestrians, and highest where there are the greatest number of cars, along Dorchester. Visitors must enter the podium to gain access to the offices above but, once inside the Complexe, it is difficult to locate the elevator cores buried within the labyrinth of retail outlets.

Determined to hire French-Canadian architects, planners, and engineers for the development, the Desjardins Movement and its partners, the Société de Développement Immobilier du Québec (SODEVIQ) rejected the widespread practice of the big Canadian banks of importing established American architects to design their corporate headquarters. Because of this practice, few local firms had had experience in planning and designing projects of such complexity and magnitude. Ultimately, the project lacks the single-minded stylishness typical of Canadian bank headquarters.

Complexe Desjardins was master-planned by one urban design firm, La Société La Haye-Ouellet, and designed in segments by a team of local architectural firms. Longpré, Marchand, Goudreau did the podium and the infrastructure for the Complexe; Blouin Blouin joined Gauthier, Guité, Roy to design the three office towers; and Jean Ouellet and Jacques Reeves, of La Haye-Ouellet, designed the Méridien Hotel. Janin Construction supervised the construction, and four consulting firms were involved in the structural and mechanical engineering.

Jacques Reeves, a partner in the architectural firm Ouellet and Reeves, comments that Place Desjardins is one of the few spaces in the project to survive the design/management process in more or less original form. "When you have two architects working on something," he observes, "if one presents the idea of doing something square, the other will obviously want to make it circular, because the pride of the firm is not to be dictated to, but to find a unique solution." Critical of the office towers' design, he was also disappointed by the materials and finishes used for the Place: "The most successful part of the Complexe is the size — not the treatment — of the interior Place. The nicest Complexe Desjardins is the one that's in the drawers."

Figure 119. Complexe Desjardins, Montreal. Escalator down to Place in foreground.

Figure 120. View of temporary photography exhibit in the Place (wood sculpture by the escalator by Pierre Grange, is a permanent installation).

Figure 121. Place Desjardins during Full Moon Friday spectacular.

Many of Montreal's public squares are of humble origin. St. Louis Square, initially a reservoir, was converted to a park in 1880 when houses were built around it. Place Victoria was a hay market, Dominion Square a cemetery, and Viger Square a swamp used as a repository for dust swept from city streets.

Place Desjardins, however, will probably never attain the international landmark status that early promotional brochures promised: "The Complexe Desjardins will be to Montreal what Times Square is to New York, what the Rond-Point of the Champs-Elysées is to Paris, and what the Picadilly Circus is to London." The social goals of the Place, as combined with the commercial goals of the Complexe, have not been smoothed over with elegant or innovative design. The expression of these goals in a characterless architectural form only points to the subordinate role in which Canadian architects have often been placed by corporate, high-rise development.

Commerce Court, Toronto

Commerce Court in Toronto is an example of a recent large development which successfully provides for private and public interests by assigning them distinct architectural forms (I. M. Pei in association with Page and Steele, 1972). Located at the southeast corner of King and Bay streets, at the ''MINT corner,'' Commerce Court is the headquarters for the Canadian Imperial Bank of Commerce. (MINT is the acronym of the four chartered banks — Montreal, Canadian-Imperial, Nova Scotia, Toronto-Dominion — with high-rise head offices quartered there.) The Commerce's L-shaped site extends south from King to Wellington Street and east from Bay to Jordan Street. *(Figures 122, 123)*

When the Bank of Commerce outgrew its headquarters building at the corner of King and Jordan in the 1960's, it chose not to demolish its office tower but to expand by assembling adjacent property. A timely amalgamation with the Imperial Bank, whose head office was a few doors down on King Street, meant that the bank owned two important corner sites in the heart of the financial district. By 1968, all eight unwanted buildings within the L-shaped assembly, including an architecturally-distinguished branch of the Bank of Nova Scotia, were demolished and parts of Jordan and Melinda streets closed.

The decision to keep the Commerce's old office tower (York & Sawyer in association with Darling and Pearson, 1931) proved to be a key move. The finely-detailed limestone tower set the tone and influenced the scale and relationships of the three new buildings that were to be constructed.

The existing tower was set off by the demolition of an adjoining building, and the base of its western side, formerly a brick party wall, was rebuilt to match the original stonework. A new arched window and door were set into the wall, and the new limestone was selected and carved to match the original. *(Figure 124)*

To differentiate the new tower, Commerce Court West, from the earlier stone building, I. M. Pei placed it so that while both have equal frontage on King Street, the new tower is set back to provide pedestrians an unobstructed view of the historical building's reconstructed west wall.

Figure 122. View, from the east, of Toronto's financial district, photographed when Commerce Court West was the tallest building downtown.

Figure 123. Site plan of Commerce Court, Toronto. All but 25
King Street West by I. M. Pei with Page and Steele, Architects.

This new 57-storey tower, like the older tower, enjoyed the distinction, when it was first built, of being the tallest building in the Commonwealth and boasted the latest in elevator, insulation, heating and life safety systems. Its curtain wall is made of sheets of stainless steel approximately sixteen metres (fifty-two feet) long, 1.2 metres (four feet) high, and three millimetres (an eighth of an inch) thick. They have "the proportions of a strip of paper," explained Oscar Duskes, the bank's project leader. Every effort, from specially devised finishes for the steel to the use of special suction machinery to lift the panels onto the structural frame without scratching them, was taken to ensure that the glass and steel of Commerce Court West would rise in a perfectly smooth sweep, in studied contrast to the masonry details of the 1931 tower adjacent. The new tower's slightly reflective windows also serve to mirror the older tower. *(Figures 125, 126)*

The other two new buildings (Commerce Court South and Commerce Court East) are clad in large limestone panels to match the older building, and kept relatively low (five and fourteen storeys) to conform to adjacent buildings on Wellington and Melinda streets. All the buildings are grouped around the centrepiece of the development, the outdoor court for which the project was named. The central court is rectangular, with passageways to streets at its four corners. Wide, shallow stairs lead up to the court, gently accommodating the slight rise in elevation of the Bay Street edge, and creating a variety of levels within the granite-paved area. Planted with honey locust trees and featuring a vast circular fountain, the Court is a welcome oasis for the buildings' occupants. The daytime population of the complex is 15,000, the equivalent of a small city. Much larger and better-lit than the narrow streets it replaces, yet more defined and sheltered than the open plaza at the neighbouring Toronto-Dominion Centre, the Court provides an urbane and accessible space well-scaled for its seasonally heavy use. *(Figure 127)*

Victor Ross, the Commerce's official historian, observed that: "In the early days the customer sought the bank, and this simplified the problem of providing premises . . . . With the development of the country and of banking came an increase of competition, and the demand that the convenience and comfort of customers should receive fuller consideration." Commerce Court is perhaps the best example among developer-sponsored public spaces of the "fuller consideration" that must be given if architecture is to address the common good.

Technological changes are largely responsible for the subtle but significant changes bank architecture has

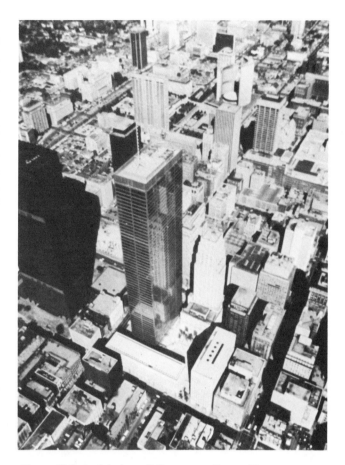

Figure 124. Aerial view of Commerce Court, Toronto.

Figure 125. (left) New Tower, Commerce Court West, Toronto. I. M. Pei with Page and Steele, Architects.

Figure 126. (below) Commerce Court. View of the court looking west, showing the fountain and the West and North towers.

Figure 127. (opposite, above) Commerce Court North (formerly called 25 King Street West). Demolition of an adjoining building exposed the brick west wall, viewed here after being clad in stone to match the other exterior walls.

Figure 128. (opposite, below) The Banking Hall in Commerce Court West.

undergone in recent years. The image of vault-like massiveness and security typical of colonnaded stone banks of the nineteenth century has evolved into a sleek, ethereal aesthetic. This is especially true in Commerce Court's new banking hall, where colossal beams and columns appear to be dematerialized by the faintly lustrous finish of their steel surfaces. Uninterrupted glass walls, glass revolving doors, glass-sided escalators, and light-coloured stone seem to attenuate the building's true mass: the base of the new tower makes tangible the bank's wish to appear accessible.

While the banking hall appears light and even informal, the development consolidates three city blocks that previously accommodated half a dozen different buildings and their respective businesses. Where the compact, fortress-like mass of a colonnaded entry used to be considered to convey stability, today extensive frontage on main streets is the means by which the competitive power of the banks is expressed. *(Figure 128)*

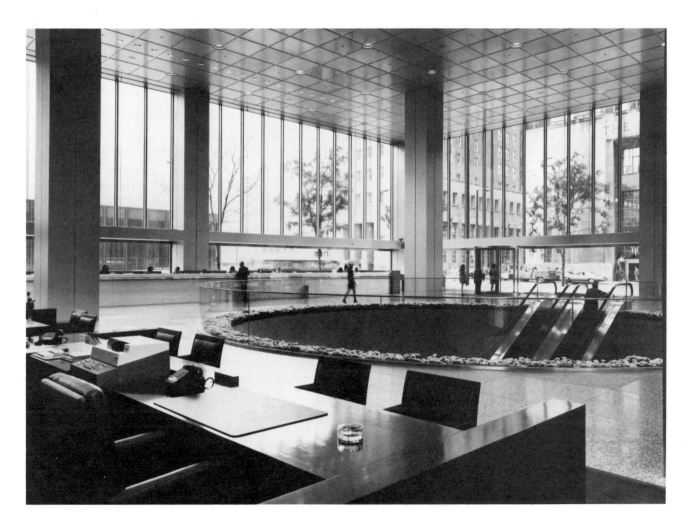

North Vancouver Civic Centre

A renewed concern for the meaning of collective life, although increasingly evident in the large-scale projects, is seen in sharpest focus in institutions recently built in smaller communities. North Vancouver's Civic Centre, the Alberta Government Services Centre, Ponoka, and the St. Boniface Cathedral, Winnipeg, all implicitly address the issues of cultural and architectural continuity on a local, recognizable scale. While not subject to the complex factors involved in the larger urban developments, these modest community institutions nevertheless indicate the extent of new, often conflicting pressures shaping the urban environment.

The use of nature as a point of reference for architecture is typical of west coast design. The tradition of making buildings relate to nature stems from the wooden structures of the Coastal Indians' settlements, and has been modified over the years by the contact Vancouver architects have had with the work of architects on the American west coast, notably those of the San Francisco Bay Area.

Founded and developed primarily for privately-owned houses, the nature-based aesthetic of the west coast has been applied to a public building with considerable success in the North Vancouver Civic Centre (Downs/Archambault, 1974). The Civic Centre bears little resemblance to the sensational, well-groomed Robson Square where landscaping has been imposed on an area of intensely-developed downtown land. Civic Centre architect Barry Downs has attempted to bring out the lush, rugged qualities that dominate the North Vancouver landscape.

Off Lonsdale Avenue between 13th and 14th streets, the new Library and City Hall complex is the present-day centre of gravity for public life in the City of North Vancouver. Founded like other parts of British Columbia on the lumber industry, North Vancouver has always been a quiet residential area. Earlier in the century, activity focussed on the waterfront. Ferries linking the town to Granville (now Vancouver's Gastown district) had their terminals at the foot of Lonsdale. Streetcars carried people up the hill to their homes.

As North Vancouver grew, its buildings spread ever farther up the hillside. Apartment towers climbed the steep and heavily-wooded north shore of Burrard Inlet vying for the best views. New highways and bridges rendered the ferry service redundant and people drove to work and to shop in mainland Vancouver rather than trolleying along Lonsdale. The end of ferry service in 1948 marked the end of the harbour as the city centre. *(Figure 129)*

Figure 129. Archival photo, streetcars and ferry docks at the foot of Lonsdale Avenue in North Vancouver.

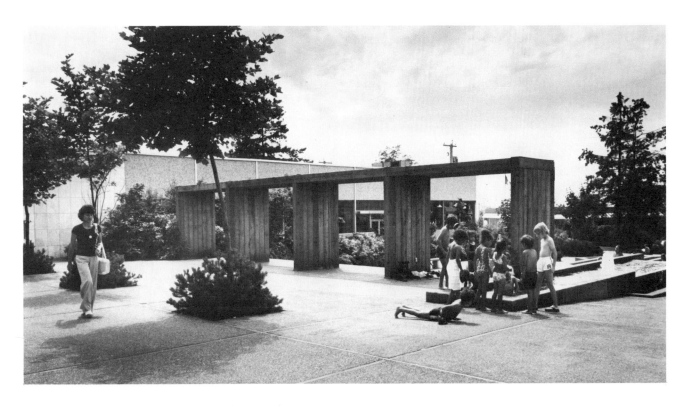

Figure 130. North Vancouver Civic Centre, looking towards the mall from Lonsdale. Rectangular wooden frames stand along the Lonsdale sidewalk where 14th street has been closed. Downs, Archambault, Architects.

Figure 131. (below) Mall at upper level of North Vancouver Civic Centre, City Hall to the right, Library to the left.

Figure 132. North Vancouver Civic Centre. Pools and fountains in the mall with City Hall in the background.

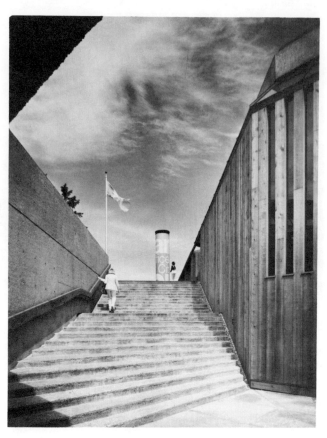

Figure 133. North Vancouver Civic Centre. Stairs from lower to upper level of mall. Stairs run parallel to the library wall, at right, which fronts on the upper mall.

When his firm was commissioned to design the new Civic Centre, which was to include both City Hall and the main library branch, Barry Downs assessed the area as formerly "one of old, rustic houses, but today most of them are gone, unfortunately. Towers dominate the site and walk-ups are all over the place. We wanted the new buildings to look comfortable on their site, and offer most of their ground to civic park space." Thus the two new concrete-frame buildings, like houses in the area, are clad in wood; they are scaled sympathetically to neighbouring low apartment blocks and offer landscaped terraces for the apartment towers to gaze down upon.

The new civic buildings are connected to the shopping area on Lonsdale by an open-air pedestrian mall made by fencing off the part of 14th Street that runs into Lonsdale. London Plane trees and square timber frames, similar to those used as sunscreens on the Civic Centre buildings, stand along the Lonsdale sidewalk where the street has been closed. *(Figure 130)*

The mall follows the contours of an extended fountain, whose terraced pools become wider and more shallow as they near the Civic Centre buildings, an allusion to the mountain streams that are one of the main geographical features of the area. The walls of the low commercial buildings on either side of the open part of 14th Street provide a shield against the ever-present car traffic, creating an informal backyard atmosphere in keeping with the community's relaxed way of life. *(Figures 131, 132, 133)*

The two civic buildings have been sited so that from the lower residential street they present a continuous jagged profile, seemingly growing out of the surrounding hill. Timber sunscreens cover the south walls of both buildings as well as the north wall of City Hall. The west side of City Hall is concealed from an adjacent walk-up by a tall stand of trees, and a berm, sheltering a quiet outdoor reading patio, hides the south side of the Library. *(Figures 134, 135)*

Figure 134. North Vancouver Civic Centre. View of City Hall (left) and Library (right) from lower level of mall.

Figure 135. North Vancouver Civic Centre. View between library (right) and City Hall (left) looking to the stairs in Figure 133.

Figure 136. North Vancouver Civic Centre. Interior of library.

Figure 137. North Vancouver Civic Centre. Interior of City Hall.

Visual and spatial variety inside the buildings is achieved by the irregular placement of walls, clerestory windows, and ceilings. Gerry Brewer, who was Director of the City's Purchasing and Property Services when the Centre was being designed, explained, "We didn't go in for different levels, from good stuff to junk, because we didn't want people confronted with sudden change as they moved through the building — to feel they'd gotten into the Executive branch because there was a carpet on the floor." *(Figures 136, 137)*

Some twenty years earlier, Ottawa, Hamilton, and Edmonton, to name only a few cities, built city halls featuring pod-like council chambers jutting out from typically modern office buildings set in broad, open plazas. By contrast, North Vancouver's Civic Centre, with its council chamber deep at its centre and its exterior sunscreens, blends so thoroughly into its setting that it is easy to drive by without noticing its presence. Its identity as a civic centre can only be sensed, since it has not been symbolized. *(Figure 138)*

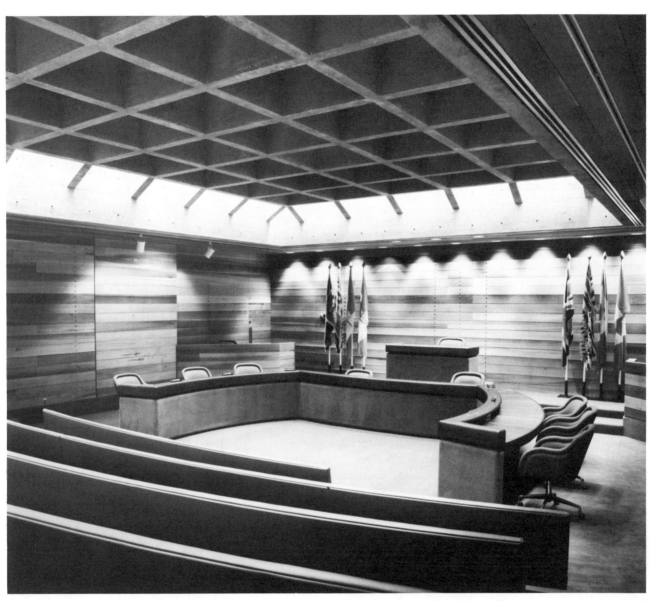

Figure 138. North Vancouver Civic Centre. Interior of Council Chamber in City Hall.

The Alberta Government Services Centre, Ponoka

The Alberta Government Services Centre in Ponoka reflects both the graceful natural forms of the surrounding rural countryside and the grass-roots policy of its Conservative client. The provincial government decided to give the sagging profile of the small town, (population, 5000) and that of its own decentralization policy, a boost by locating several of its facilities there in a new building, with the Alberta Opportunity Company as the primary tenant. The Company was set up to make loans to small businesses that cannot secure loans from conventional sources.

The mandate to design a building that would aggrandize the government's presence in the town was implicit. As Ed Clarke, the managing director of the Alberta Opportunity Company, put it:

> The members of the Cabinet said, in effect, to the Department of Public Works, ''We want to make a very strong statement. We want to have a dramatic building in this small community of Ponoka to reemphasize to the people of Alberta our commitment to putting operations of the government in small towns wherever it is feasible.'' So for that reason Doug Cardinal was called in because his qualifications as a dramatic designer I think are well known.

Undeniably dramatic, the Services Centre designed by architect Douglas J. Cardinal is perhaps best described as a series of events, of restlessly fluid forms defying attempts to locate a visual focus. Walls seem to be pulled out of each other, others seem to be drawn right out of the ground, creating the impression of smaller buildings growing out of the larger one. The building's episodic, de-centralized character draws attention to it as a somewhat alien presence in the life of the town. To one side is a commercial strip replete with a 7-Eleven store; on the other is a street of modest wood-frame houses. Facing the Centre is another street of wooden houses, while behind it, across a lane, is the local lumber yard.

The customary design solution of providing a principal facade, to be regarded from one static, central position, was ruled out from the start. ''One facade,'' says Doug Cardinal, ''would [have made the building] look like a train, a three-storey train. By pulling stairwells and forms in and out, when you walk down the sidewalk, you get a series of experiences, rather than just one — blah — government building experience.'' *(Figures 139, 140)*

Figure 139. First Floor Plan of Alberta Government Services Centre, Ponoka. Douglas J. Cardinal, architect.

Figure 140. Model of Alberta Government Services Centre, Ponoka.

At either end of the building two cylindrical pavilions curve tantalizingly away from view. Inside, both pavilions are perfectly circular in plan, with ceilings formed like a wheel with spokes radiating out from a hub. The western one is a court room. Here the centre point is the place where the accused and counsel sit. The eastern pavilion, which faces the commercial strip, is a branch of the Alberta government credit union. As in the court room, the visitor's glance is drawn to the centre of the space, but here tellers, not the accused, occupy the central area.

Outside, the cylindrical forms of the pavilions blend into the undulating main body of the building. The back and front form a continuous, over-all facade, inverting the typical function of end pavilions. In Neoclassical institutional buildings, end pavilions tend to draw attention to the monumental aspects of the central hall, while in Cardinal's building, their effect is to deformalize the entire structure. Furthermore, Cardinal's symbolically introverted forms belie the fact that most of the building's interior is devoted to quite ordinary government office space, grouped around a quite ordinary, though curvilinear, central atrium. *(Figures 141, 142)*

Structurally, the curvilinearity of the Alberta Government Services Centre would have been most easily executed in concrete, and it would have been in keeping with local building conventions to have used stucco as a finishing material. But Cardinal sought instead to approximate the limitless subtlety one finds on the Prairies as the sun passes over the narrow range of colours and forms. And so, to make the building's surface more analogous to the natural surroundings, and despite the difficulties it posed for construction, the architect insisted on cladding it in variegated brick, which changes colour with the weather, and throughout the day as the sun strikes it from different angles. Thus it is difficult to attribute a single nature to this building, or to take its measure with a single glance.

Unlike the simply-constructed traditional buildings of the Prairies, such as the grain elevators at the foot of the street Cardinal's building sits on, the Government Services Centre has been achieved with an astonishing array of technological props, from computers to Crazy Glue. Computers facilitated the complex calculations necessitated by the irregular structural forms, and Crazy Glue was applied to keep recalcitrant bricks in place. The result is a structure quite different from vernacular buildings of the Prairies which, like the grain elevators, most often make their presence felt as acts of defiance to the subtly amorphous nature of the landscape. By contrast, Cardinal's unorthodox building looks as though it had been blown and eroded into shape by natural forces. *(Figure 143)*

Figure 141. Exterior of Alberta Government Services Centre, showing steps leading to main entrance of the government offices. Douglas J. Cardinal, architect.

Figure 142. Alberta Government Services Centre, Interior, atrium.

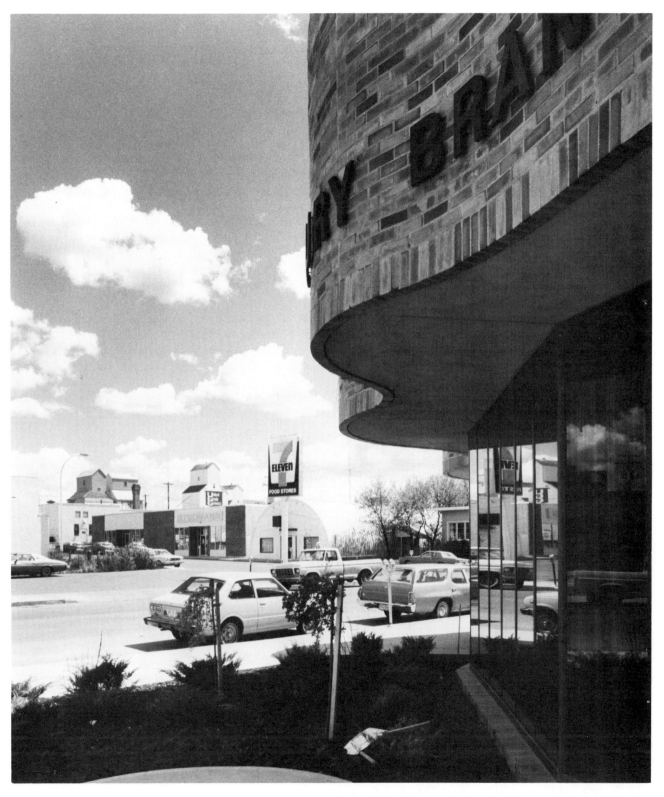

Figure 143. The Alberta Government Services Centre, view of Ponoka from sidewalk beside the Treasury Branch.

St. Boniface Cathedral, Winnipeg

The evolution of a community's cultural traditions is epitomized by the reconstruction of St. Boniface Cathedral, the fifth cathedral to be built on a magnificent site facing the Red River in Manitoba's main French-speaking settlement. The first cathedral was built of logs in 1819 by Father Provencher, the first Bishop of Western Canada. The second, larger cathedral was destroyed by fire in 1860. The third cathedral was the scene of Louis Riel's funeral in 1885, and was demolished after the fourth and largest cathedral, a Tyndall limestone structure, was completed directly behind it. Riel, who was born in St. Boniface, is buried in the graveyard in front of the fourth cathedral, beside his relatives the Lagimodières, the first white family to settle in Western Canada. Foundation stones from the corners of the third cathedral are still visible amongst the graves. In 1968, workmen repairing the roof of the sixty-year-old building inadvertently started a fire which quickly gutted the body of the basilica, leaving only the outer walls and fragments of the curved wall of the sanctuary. *(Figure 144)*

When, in 1970, the City of St. Boniface was amalgamated with other communities to form a "unicity" government for Winnipeg, many citizens feared that their long-standing control over their French-speaking institutions was in jeopardy. This sudden secular change followed the more gradual ecumenical ones introduced by Pope John XXIII's Second Vatican Council, which started in the early sixties. These changes involved fundamental transformations of Roman Catholic liturgy that were meant to inspire a direct, fraternal relationship between man and God in the religious service, by de-emphasizing the elaborate intermediary symbols which had evolved over the centuries.

By the time of the 1968 fire, the diocese recognized that the building would have to be altered to accommodate the new, democratized liturgy. Although only the outer walls were left, many people, nevertheless, were tempted to build the cathedral anew. However, by 1970, the cost of an accurate reconstruction proved beyond the reach of the congregation, which was only half as large as the one for which the old cathedral had been built. They chose the firm of Etienne J. Gaboury and Associates to make proposals for a replacement.

While the way in which the cathedral was rebuilt reflected the community's quest to implement the directives of the Second Vatican Council, it also represented a significant change in its architect's approach to the design of religious buildings, and perhaps to architecture generally. Etienne Gaboury, a Franco-Manitoban architect who has designed all types of institutional buildings in St. Boniface, is perhaps best known for his

Figure 144. A view across the Red River to the stone frontispiece of the old St. Boniface Cathedral, St. Boniface, Manitoba.

religious buildings such as the Paroisse du Précieux Sang (Precious Blood), which radically altered the way people experienced religious services. The unusual formal organization of his churches — the plan of Precious Blood is spiral — jolted the congregation into direct, often austere, relationship to the religious service.

In the case of the St. Boniface Cathedral, however, the idea of removing the former building's traces so as to build a smaller, modern cathedral would have meant going backwards historically, in that previously, each successive cathedral built on the site had been larger than its predecessor. It was imperative, as far as Etienne Gaboury was concerned, to incorporate fragments of the former building in a contemporary cathedral. *(Figure 145)*

One can still approach the building by entering the white, wrought-iron gate on Taché Avenue, and continuing along the sidewalk that bisects the graveyard. At the end of the sidewalk rises the limestone facade of the old Cathedral. The turrets of its towers were destroyed in the fire, making the highest point the cross at its centre. Below the cross, the circular opening of a former rose window startlingly reveals the sky, and, gradually as one continues along the sidewalk, the vast, rusted steel roof of the new building. *(Figure 146)*

Figure 145. Model of the Diocese of St. Boniface, numbered buildings have been designed or renovated by Etienne Gaboury. No. 1 is the St. Boniface Cathedral.

Figure 146. St. Boniface Cathedral. A frontal view of the old cathedral's face, the roof of the new cathedral seen through the opening of what was once a rose window.

Figure 147. Site plan of the St. Boniface Cathedral reconstruction. Shaded area shows extent of roof of the new cathedral. Etienne Gaboury, Architect.

Figure 148. Main Floor Plan of St. Boniface Cathedral reconstruction.

a Baptismal Font	e Holy Reserve	i Ambo	D Sanctuary	G Discussion	K Coat Room	O Vestibule
b Lectern	f Organ Pipes	A Atrium	E Bishops'	H Work Sacristy	L Collection Rm	P Workshop
c Sedilia	g Confessionals	B Narthex	Sacristy	I Office	M Womens' W.C.	Q Dressing Room
d Altar	h Organ Console	C Nave: 1000 p	F Catechism Rm	J Caretaker	N Mens' W.C.	

Figure 149. St. Boniface Cathedral. Section through the new building showing its relation to the remains of the old.

The long, narrow dimensions of the former building did not readily lend themselves to a contemporary Roman Catholic church service — ideally, a square or circular space where the congregation gathers in an intimate and uncomplicated relationship to the altar. Taking both the long processional route of the old, and the compact space of the new into consideration, Etienne Gaboury inserted a square contemporary cathedral into the well-preserved sanctuary still standing at the rear of the site. The area between the back of the impressive, now windowless front wall of the old cathedral and the modest low front wall of the new cathedral was retained in its roofless fragmentary state. This outdoor courtyard now functions as a lobby, a sheltered space for the socializing that precedes and concludes religious services. *(Figures 147, 148, 149)*

In this courtyard, the relationship between the old and new cathedrals becomes clear. Where once there were aisles, there now stand six new column-like objects of the same self-rusting steel as the new cathedral's roof. The self-rusting steel, evoking the structure that was destroyed in the fire, symbolizes the common properties of the ruin and the new buildings, as do the large blocks of stone which have been rescued from the old walls and placed randomly, as benches, before the threshold of the new cathedral. These elements help to make the courtyard a place of transition between the former cathedral's ceremonial approach and the more domestic qualities of the new building. *(Figures 150, 151, 152, 153)*

Rather than revolutionizing the progression of spaces inside the new cathedral as he had in previous churches, Gaboury modelled the plan after early Roman basilicas in which the relationship between the nave and the sanctuary at the rear is simple and direct. The new sanctuary, wedged into the remnants of the one left standing after the fire, retains its simple cylindrical form. The square-shaped body of the building accommodates a glassed-in porch-like reception area (the narthex) and the cathedral proper. Gone is the traditional choir loft with its long row of confessional booths underneath. The choir, when it is present, joins the rest of the congregation, sitting in pews at the front. Confessionals are small office-like rooms projecting out from both sides of the body of the cathedral. The apse, where the long axis culminates, has been cleared of the many devotional and immobile objects that typically furnished sanctuaries in nineteenth-century churches. *(Figure 154)*

Neither an exact replica nor a revolutionary statement about the building it replaced, the new St. Boniface Cathedral holds great cultural significance for its community. It is a work of restraint, reflecting the persistence of local traditions while representing current practice in Catholic worship. Like the Alberta Government Services Centre and the North Vancouver Civic Centre, the Cathedral bears witness to the aspirations of the community it serves.

Figure 150. St. Boniface Cathedral. Exterior view of new cathedral and of side entrance to courtyard through ruined wall of the old. Etienne Gaboury, Architect.

Figure 151. St. Boniface Cathedral. View back across courtyard to frontispiece of the old cathedral.

Figure 152. St. Boniface Cathedral. View from ruined stair tower across the courtyard to the new cathedral.

Figure 153. St. Boniface Cathedral. View of courtyard and new cathedral.

THE CHANGING FORMS OF PUBLIC LIFE 139

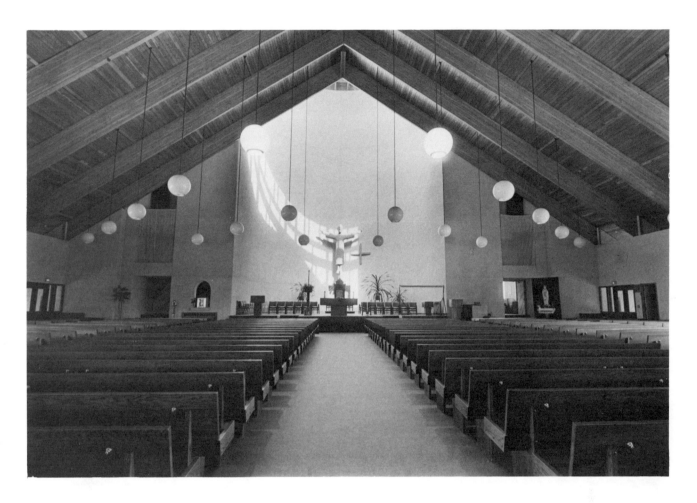

Figure 154. Interior of new St. Boniface Cathedral, St. Boniface.

A growing recognition of the value of inner-city sites and existing buildings is in evidence in much of the new construction in Canadian cities. Comparison of these community-scale projects with the same architects' work of the 1960's — aggressively isolated projects like the Simon Fraser campus by Arthur Erickson and Geoffrey Massey, (Burnaby, B.C.), Douglas Cardinal's St. Mary's Church, (Red Deer, Alberta), Eberhard Zeidler's McMaster Health Sciences Centre, (Hamilton, Ontario), Etienne Gaboury's Precious Blood Church, (Winnipeg, Manitoba) — show how profound the re-evaluation of urban design has been.

In buildings and projects of widely differing scales, these architects have abandoned many of the reductive characteristics of the immediate post-War period. In moving away from the earlier goal of producing neutral backgrounds adaptable to every function, architects are making specific accommodations for the shifts in contemporary culture.

V Change and Continuity: Towards a Reconciliation

More and more in recent years, have we seen profound criticism and questioning of the precepts of International Style architecture. While many talented and well-established architects find it convenient to label all alternative approaches ''Post-Modernism,'' and to condemn them as effete and socially irrelevant, the fundamental facts are that the International Style has been damaging to the urban environment and that the public continues to find it, on the whole, unengaging and uninspiring.

Moving beyond the ''two-camps'' approach of Modernism and Post-Modernism, which remains a superficial explanation of current architectural thought, many architects have attempted to combine the sometimes conflicting aims of the founding ideals of Modern Architecture with the more recent movements towards a socially and environmentally conservative architecture. Architecture, in this case, is intended to be neither strikingly new, nor purely a reflection of that which went before, but to occupy a middle ground between the two.

As part of this trend, a new Canadian architecture is emerging. Its creators draw on the freedom of forms, materials and spaces inherent in the idea of a modern architecture, while also responding to the existing physical and cultural context. Some of the best of these buildings are discussed in this chapter. They bode well for the future: here is an architecture not only optimistic and forward-looking, but also firmly rooted in local and public traditions.

Museum of Anthropology, Vancouver

Not many of Arthur Erickson's buildings are good examples of this recent trend. Canada's best-known architect views much of today's culture as "trash-oriented," and therefore ignores it. As a result, many of his large urban projects, such as Vancouver's Robson Square and Toronto's new Roy Thomson Hall, seem detached from their surroundings. But, where Erickson does value the context, he responds quite differently and carefully to the surrounding environment. A case in point is his design for Vancouver's Museum of Anthropology (Arthur Erickson Architects, 1975).

Perhaps more than anything else, Arthur Erickson is enamoured of the richness and beauty of the British Columbia landscape. His Robson Square suggests a lush, eventful, natural landscape in the middle of downtown Vancouver. Such efforts, however, were unnecessary in the magnificent natural setting acquired for the Museum of Anthropology. Perched on the Point Grey Cliffs of the campus of the University of British Columbia, the rear of the site affords a panorama of Howe Sound below, and the mountains of the North Shore in the distance. *(Figure 155)*

Figure 155. Site Plan, Museum of Anthropology, University of British Columbia, Vancouver. Arthur Erickson, Architect.

From the parking lot, however, the vista is almost completely concealed by a large berm. A chunk of this vast earthwork has been removed to reveal the museum's grand front entrance. Like the berm, which conceals most of the building only to reveal and emphasize its entrance, the museum conceals and then reveals the site as the visitor passes through. *(Figure 156)* "Since the site is sloped," explains Erickson of the way the building structures the visitor's passage through the site, "I felt that the whole movement should be down a long ramp, with more and more revealed, until the whole space burst open with a view of the sea."

From the lobby a carpeted ramp, lined with larger-than-life Northwest Coast Indian wood statues, leads down to the rear of the building. At the bottom, the passageway suddenly opens up into the dramatic, windowed Great Hall, where the museum's extraordinary collection of totem poles stands against a backdrop of forest, water and mountains. *(Figures 157, 158)*

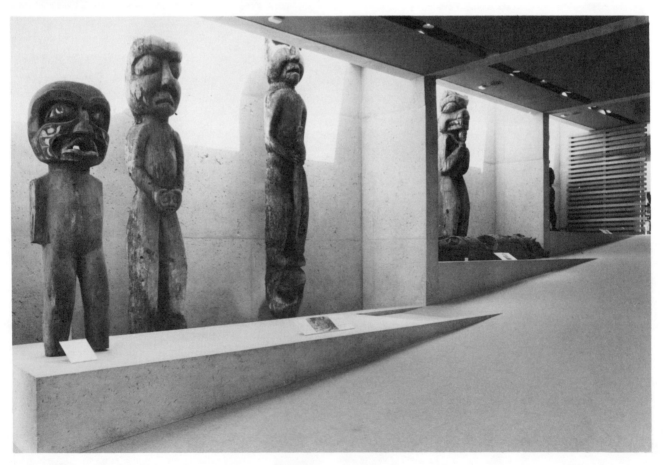

Figures 156, 157. Museum of Anthropology, the grand front entrance (above) and (below) a carpeted ramp which leads down to the rear of the building.

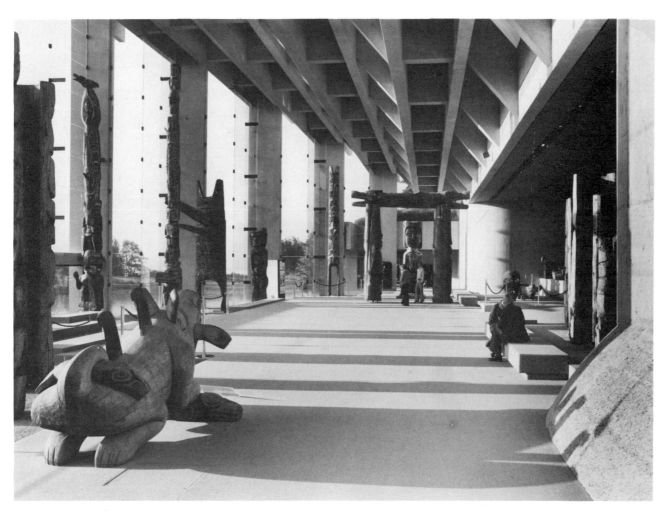

Figure 158. Museum of Anthropology. Interior view of the Great Hall: ". . . down a long ramp . . . until the whole space burst open with a view of the sea." (Erickson).

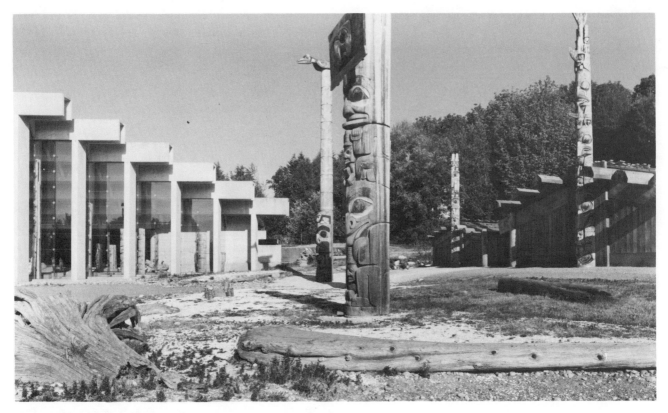

Figures 159, 160. The major structural theme of the museum recalls the forms of the early Haida houses.

Built to house the University of British Columbia's sizable collection of Northwest Coast Indian art, the Museum of Anthropology reflects in many ways the artifacts it contains. "When I was designing the museum," explains Erickson, "I remembered a photograph of an early Indian village between the edge of the forest and the edge of the sea." Accordingly, Erickson created a path for a river at the rear of the site, and located not only his building but also two of the museum's recreated Haida log houses along it. (The pebbled path has yet to be filled with water because of environmental objections raised by the university.)

Looking back from the rear of the site at the Great Hall and the two Haida houses, the first and most obvious relationship is in the resemblance between the simple and powerful forms of the museum and those of the houses. A closer look at the museum and the culture of the Northwest Coast peoples reveals other, more subtle similiarities. *(Figure 159)*

Beginning at the entrance, the visitor is introduced to the major formal or structural theme of the building. The museum is constructed of a series of frames or

Figure 161. Museum of Anthropology, looking inland at the Great Hall: architecture which structures and heightens the visitors perceptions. Arthur Erickson, Architect.

gates, each unit consisting of a horizontal beam supported by two vertical posts. Although a single gate or frame would have marked the entrance to a typical Northwest Coast Indian log house, in the museum they are used in sets; three, for instance, are used to create the main entrance to the building.

Each of these frames has a carefully-differentiated front face and side profile, a distinction also important to the art of the Northwest Coast Indians, wherein animals are traditionally painted either in full face or side profile according to which view is thought to best portray a creature's most salient characteristics. The face of the shark, for example, is always shown from the front, fully capturing its powerful teeth. The raven, with its pronounced beak, is almost always shown in profile. In the museum, the face of each gate — the plane through which one walks — is represented by a deep beam sitting on two slender piers; the side of the gate reveals the narrow "U"-shaped profile of the beam, resting on two wide piers. Together, these individual gates provide the museum as a whole with a face

and a profile, like a person, or a thunderbird for that matter. *(Figure 160)*

The culmination of the museum in the Great Hall is as grand from the outside as it is from the inside. Looking back at the museum from the rear of the site, the gates or frames have been arranged so that all of them will be visible. Although each gate is distinct, not one of them could be removed without destroying the overall unity of the group. Again, a parallel can be drawn with Northwest Coast Indian art, where the true forms of animals are often distorted to conform to the limits of the picture plane. Totem poles, for example, are built up out of a number of discreet, but interdependent parts. *(Figure 161)*

Few visitors fail to be moved by the museum. On the surface, it is a cool and pristine building in contrast to its lush setting and unusually animate artifacts. Fundamentally, however, the architecture of the museum structures and heightens the visitor's perceptions both of British Columbia's grand landscape and of its Northwest Coast Indian Art.

Pavilion '70, The Laurentians, Quebec

Architecturally ambitious and site sensitive, Pavilion '70 (Righter, Rose and Lankin, 1976-8) is a ski chalet located an hour north of Montreal in Quebec's Laurentian Mountains. Like the Museum of Anthropology, Pavilion '70 has an architectural character appropriate to its function. *(Figure 162)*

Movement through Pavilion '70 is casual and lacks the processional character of a walk through the museum, but there are similarities in the way that the two buildings contract and expand according to external circumstance. The side of Pavilion '70 facing the parking lot is compact and condensed *(Figure 163)*. A central recessed door leads into an unremarkable central hallway lined with metal lockers for skiers. A large stair on the left leads up and out to the main floor of the building. There a central hall gives way to a semi-circular, exterior court opening out towards the ski slopes at the rear of the site.

Figure 162. Site Plan and Site Section of Pavilion '70, a ski lodge in the Laurentians an hour north of Montreal. Righter, Rose and Lankin, Architects.

Figure 163. Pavilion '70, elevation facing the parking lot with the ski-hill rising behind.

Figure 164. Pavilion '70, elevation facing the slopes, the symmetry of the facade and the semi-circular court provide an image both grand and inviting. Righter, Rose and Lankin, Architects.

To skiers gliding down towards it, Pavilion '70's symmetrical wood-clad facade presents an image of grandness that belies the actual size of the building. Visual interest is focussed at the centre of the building, on the chalet's formal exterior court and entrance. The semi-circular court serves as a transitional area, a bridge between the scale of the ski-hill and that of the lodge's interior. The curved wood arcade, which defines the court, houses a continuous bench which is warmed by radiant heaters concealed within the uppermost part of the structure. Skiers use these seats at the beginning and end of their day, to put skis on and take them off. Those who prefer not to risk a broken leg or frostbite have a perfect perch from which to watch. A balcony off the second floor bar provides both a canopy and a rather theatrical platform from which to observe the forecourt below and the ski-hills above. *(Figure 164)*

There is something familiar but also exotic about the form of the lodge: it is, at once, a barn, a Quebec manor house and an Italian villa. Wood is the primary structural and cladding material, and it is also used wherever the hand comes into contact with the building, for doorpulls, interior wainscotting, moulding and trim. Pastel colours in recesses throughout the building contrast with the natural wood surfaces of the main walls, imparting an interesting, layered effect to much of the interior. An easy charm pervades the pavilion, and the building is an accommodating and colourful host to the skiers who come from all over the world to use it. *(Figures 165, 166)*

Figure 165, 166. The easy charm of Pavilion '70's interior.

Gaslight Square, Vancouver

In a rural setting, architectural issues are easier to isolate, and architectural ambitions tend to be less compromised than in an urban one. In cities, sites and constraints are tighter, and political influences are more complex. As discussed previously, urban buildings are often designed by committees, and unfortunately often tend to look that way. Urban buildings which conserve and enhance their surroundings, without either disappearing into them or overpowering them, are rare. Four such buildings are discussed below.

As of the mid-60s, the plan for much of Vancouver's waterfront could be summed up by the term Project 200. Conceived as a way of upgrading one of the city's most run-down areas, Project 200 was named for its estimated cost, in 1965, of $200 million. A project of this magnitude was only possible because of Marathon Realty's ability to make available the CPR railyards along Vancouver's waterfront, which it owned, to a development consortium, Project 200 Properties.

Associated with Project 200 was a highway planned to cut through the old waterfront district and adjacent Chinatown. Both the highway and Project 200 provoked considerable protest from citizens' groups. An alternative proposal prepared by the architectural firm of Birmingham and Wood, argued in a detailed and persuasive way for retention and restoration of the historic waterfront district of Gastown. Some new businesses and shops had recently established themselves in the area and some renovation was already underway. With encouragement from city council, the province declared Gastown an historic site, thereby putting an end to the possibility of indiscriminate demolition in the area.

By 1973, Project 200 had been scrapped. But rather than sell its historic block of buildings on Water Street, the consortium chose to hire the firm of Henriquez and Todd to prepare a redevelopment plan for that block alone.

Henriquez and Todd presented a three-stage development plan for the almost 180-metre-long (approximately 600-foot-long) Water Street block. In the first stage, an empty lot in the middle of the block was to become a public square. The new square would be defined by the two existing warehouse buildings flanking the lot, and by a new retail and office building placed between the lot and the street. In the second stage, the block's other buildings were to be restored and new signs and awnings installed. The third phase called for the renovation of upper floor warehouse spaces for use as offices and housing to meet expected demand. *(Figure 167)*

For the public square, the client initially envisioned a "U"-shaped building, its forecourt opening onto the street in the manner of a typical suburban shopping mall. The architects disagreed, however, insisting that such a solution would destroy the continuity of the existing buildings' facades.

Now determined to do the right thing for the community, Project 200 Properties consented to the Henriquez and Todd design for the square. Rather than the broad opening to the square envisioned by the client, the architect's design called for a carefully defined courtyard entered through a small gap between the facades of the new and old buildings. Completed by 1975, and named Gaslight Square, the three-building complex maintains the continuity of the street's facades, as well as the integrity of the block and area generally.

The street facade of Gaslight Square is dominated by the new building, which is wider and taller than the renovated commercial buildings to either side. Like the existing commercial buildings, the ground floor of the new building features stores with large display windows. Striped canvas awnings shelter the sidewalk in front of the shops. Above the shops is general office space, and a brick facade which features six oriel windows, an unusually-shaped window common to Gastown. *(Figure 168)*

Figures 167, 168. Gaslight Square, Vancouver. (At top) Site plan and (above) Water Street facade. Henriquez and Todd, Architects.

Figure 169. Gaslight Square, the Water Street facade.

Although the materials and forms of the new building are characteristic of the area, the intent of the new, in the words of Henriquez, was to "capture the spirit of what was there without copying it word for word." Thus, some elements have been exaggerated through the manipulation of size and proportion. The "wall-like" quality of the facade has been emphasized by making it wider and flatter than traditional buildings in the area, and through the absence of mouldings and detailed surface decoration. Similarly, the oriel windows are, in relation to the wall, proportionately much bigger than they would be normally. *(Figure 169)*

The square, or courtyard is now sheltered on all four sides: by the new building on the north and south sides, and by the two renovated buildings to the east and west. A walkway encircles the courtyard, gently climbing up and around it, taking the visitor on a gradual spiral tour past the shops inserted into the old structure at the first and second levels. *(Figures 170, 171)*

From its four storey street facade, the new building steps down to two storeys in the courtyard, allowing sun into the square for a longer period of the day. Views of the Burrard Inlet and the North Shore, not possible from Water Street, can be glimpsed from the courtyard's upper walkway. And in contrast to the flat and hard face that the new building presents to the street, the courtyard walls of the complex are veiled and softened by awnings and abundant planting in troughs inserted into the new building's structure. *(Figures 172, 173)*

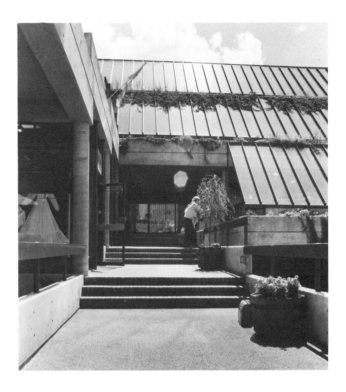

Figures 170, 171. Gaslight Square, the walkway stepping up and around the courtyard. Henriquez and Todd, Architects.

Figures 172, 173. The courtyard walls of Gaslight Square are veiled by awnings and planting, and enlivened by views of the North Shore. Henriquez and Todd, Architects.

Innis College, Toronto

It was not so much community outrage as a sagging university budget that was responsible for the modesty of the building programme of Innis College in the early 1970s. Established in 1964 as a part of the University of Toronto, Innis College was initially located in a house on Toronto's St. George Street. A few years later, the Toronto firm of Massey Flanders was retained to prepare plans for new facilities on a site along the north side of nearby Sussex Street, between St. George and Huron streets. The Massey Flanders design, approved by the college in 1968, accommodated a projected enrollment of 1500 students, 576 in residence, in a block-long development which featured a ten-storey tower at either end. In proposing to demolish the existing row of Victorian houses along the north side of Sussex Street, and to replace them with a building of a completely different scale, the Massey Flanders scheme resembled the development underway across the street. There, the design for the university's fourteen-storey Robarts Library had required demolition of an entire block. It opened in 1973, and was immediately dubbed "Fort Book" because of its mammoth scale and fortress-like character.

Unlike Robarts Library, the Massey Flanders

Figure 174. Site Plan, Innis College, the University of Toronto. Diamond and Myers, Architects; Jack Diamond, partner-in-charge.

Figure 175. The Sussex Street facade of Innis College is broken into smaller house-like forms.

scheme fell victim to university cutbacks. In June 1970, John Evans, then the president of the university, advised the college that its new complex could not be built in the "forseeable future." That decision forced a "fundamental rethinking of what the college should be" in the words of Innis College administrator Art Wood, and the college chose to remain small, keeping its projected enrollment to a maximum of 800 students.

Still, Innis required new facilities and a number of architects were interviewed before the Toronto firm of Diamond and Myers was chosen. Chief among the reasons for choosing the firm was its past involvement in community planning and its early advocacy of conservation, re-use and infilling new construction between existing buildings where possible.

In addition, there was the issue of architectural character, the image and atmosphere which would be appropriate for the college. Innis professor Joe Medjuk explains: "One architect, after reading the brief we had prepared, said to us, 'All you people really want is another house,' which was true. We had one old house, and we wanted another but with more stuff in it. As far as this went, Jack [Diamond] knew what we wanted."

As for the site, with a smaller programme and no residential component, less land was required. Both college and architect agreed to preserve the houses still standing on Sussex Street and to design any new structure to blend in with them. "Our first concern," says Joe Medjuk, "was to keep the houses."

Compared to the controversy which attended the opening of Robarts Library across the street, Innis College opened quietly on January 6, 1976. The old houses along the north side of Sussex Street were retained, and one was renovated for use by the college. Attached to this renovated house in an ingenious way is the new part of the college, which extends to the corner of Sussex and St. George streets. From Sussex Street, the complex gives the impression of three "houses," one existing house, and a new building built in two house-like forms. On the larger and busier St. George Street, the image is all new and, in keeping with this street's character, institutional rather than residential. "The first point," explains partner-in-charge Jack Diamond, "was really the restoring of a block, the knitting together of an urban fabric. There were going to be an array of urban elements. [Some never got built.] It wasn't going to be another big building." *(Figures 174, 175)*

Figure 176. Innis College, new building integrated with renovated Victorian house. Diamond and Myers, Architects; Jack Diamond, partner-in-charge.

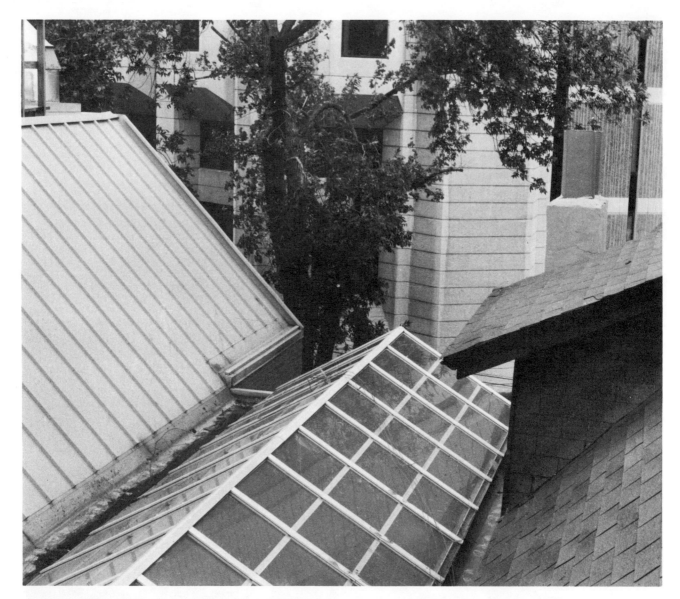

Figure 177. Innis College, glass-roofed walkways join new and old.

The two parts of the new building allude to the Victorian houses next door. They are the same height as the old ones, and, in a rudimentary way, of the same form: brick piers form an arcade reminiscent of the porches next door. Different materials are used on the upper and lower portions of the new building: while the existing house employs brick and shingles, the change on the new building is from brick to clay tile. The simplified roof lines of the new "houses" reflect the steeply pitched gables and intricate dormers of the older houses. By contrast, the shiny, fat aluminum pipes piled deliberately atop the new roof bear little resemblance to the old brick chimneys next door. *(Figures 176, 177)*

From Sussex Street, the three solid brick buildings are separated by glass-covered walkways which are set back from the brick facades so that they seem, from a cursory glance down the street, not to be there. But the walkways become highly important once one is inside the college. Access to the old house with its classrooms, offices and pub; to the central new building which is called the Town Hall; and to the administrative offices, library, and classrooms, is all via the walkways. People and natural light constantly cross horizontal and vertical paths. *(Figure 178)*

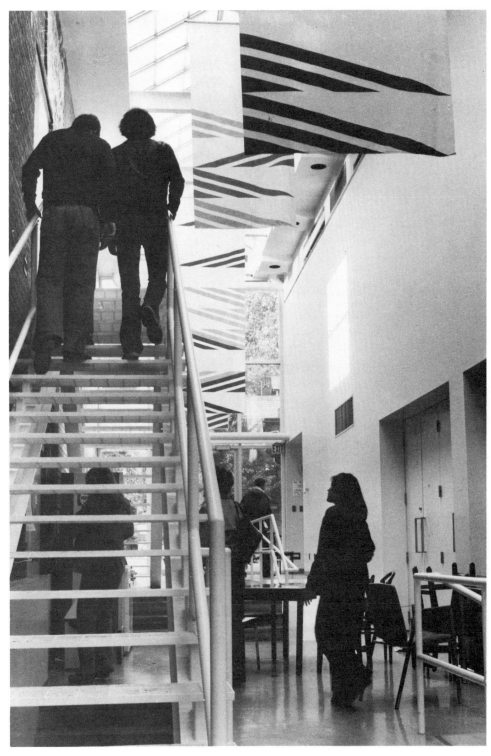

Figure 178. Innis College, access to various parts of the college is through the lively and enjoyable glass-roofed walkways. Diamond and Myers, Architects; Jack Diamond, partner-in-charge.

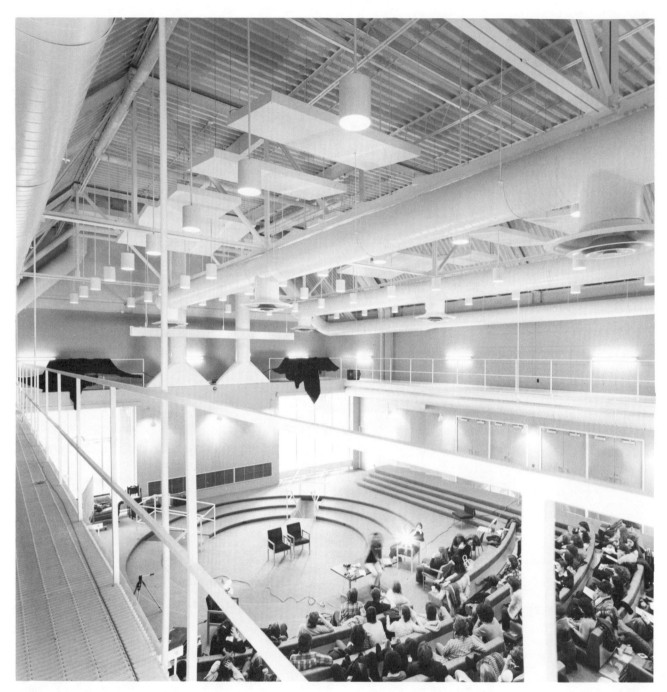

Figure 179. Innis College, the Town Hall.

Figure 180. Innis College, the library, a quiet, white refuge from the activity of the public walkways. Diamond and Myers, Architects; Jack Diamond, partner-in-charge.

Despite the straightforward organization of the interior, there is a surprising amount of spatial variety, and variety of character within the college. The heart of the college is the Town Hall. In contrast to the carefree skylit walkways that surround it with light and movement, the Town Hall is a brooding, high and dark room. Large white ducts twist under the ceiling, and flare outwards behind the catwalk over a central stage area. Below, the floor's carpeted concentric circles radiate upward from the sunken pool in the centre. "The Town Hall," explains college administrator Art Wood, "was designed to foster oral communication." And it does. "In that room," he continues, pacing back and forth in his small office, "everyone becomes a peripatetic." *(Figure 179)*

The small but airy and open library in the building's "attic" offers a quiet, white refuge from the activity and noise of the public walkways. Here, too, the use of open metal gratings, an architectural theme first introduced in the main stairs, is explored fully and with great beauty. *(Figure 180)*

One of the most popular places in the college, and, in fact, in the university as a whole, is the Innis College Pub. "We asked for a place that could be easily jammed," explains Art Wood, "and that's what we got." Smokey, low and dimly-lit, the new pub incorporates the front room of the renovated house into the college. Lamps, a fireplace and old class pictures lend a comfortably cluttered look to the old room, a dark and mysterious gem which blends in well with the rest of the pub, exemplifying the successful way in which old and new have been combined throughout the College.

Centennial Hall, Winnipeg

Innis College is part of a long tradition of important buildings which have resulted from university commissions. Looking back only so far as the 1960s, Simon Fraser University, Scarborough College, and Massey College each provided initial opportunity and exposure for, respectively, Arthur Erickson, John Andrews and Ron Thom. More recently, the Nova Scotia College of Art and Design has had a large hand in Halifax's waterfront restoration, the University of Toronto has sponsored Innis College, and the newly-formed University of Winnipeg has commissioned the visionary and yet essentially conservative Centennial Hall.

At one time simply a downtown campus of the University of Manitoba, Winnipeg's United College was given a charter of its own in the mid-1960s, and renamed the University of Winnipeg. Expanding enrollment soon necessitated larger facilities, but the newly-chartered institution owned only one block of land in downtown Winnipeg, and that block was already covered, to a large extent, by buildings of various shapes and sizes.

On the south side of the block and facing Portage Avenue, Winnipeg's main boulevard, stands Wesley Hall, a great sandstone monument. Completed in 1896, the Hall was historically identified as *the* college, and later as *the* university. Alongside and behind it are a number of two, three, and four storey buildings of various styles built between 1957 and 1964. Together Wesley Hall and the smaller buildings formed a highly-valued courtyard at the center of the block.

There was one empty plot of land on the block's north end, and that was quickly used for the university's first new building, Lockhart Hall, completed in 1969 by the Winnipeg firm of Moody Moore Duncan Rattray Peters Searle Christie (MMDRPSC). This new brick building, with its picturesque towers, anchored the nor-

Figure 181. Aerial view of University of Winnipeg campus in the late 60's, the sandstone and turreted Wesley Hall facing Portage Avenue at the southern end of the site.

thern end of the campus, complimenting the Neo-romanesque style of Wesley Hall to the south.

The university still lacked adequate classroom space, a proper library, and room to house student services. In total, it required an additional 28,000 square metres (approximately 300,000 square feet). Not only had the last remaining lot been utilized, but 28,000 metres was roughly equivalent to a building three times the size of Lockhart Hall. "Groundspace," recalls Dr. J. G. Pincock, Assistant to the President of the University, "was totally inadequate to erect anything remotely resembling that amount of square footage."

The university's choices were limited. One option was to purchase new land outside of its original block. Although there was an already-assembled, suitably large

Figure 182. Aerial view of the University of Winnipeg campus with the steel frame of Centennial Hall under construction; the completed brick Lockhart Hall (1969) is at the extreme north of the block. Moody Moore Duncan Rattray Peters Searle Christie, Architects.

site available across the street, its owner wanted double what the university could afford to pay. Another possibility was the selective demolition of some of the lower, newer buildings on the block. But then alternative facilities would have been required while the new ones were going up. With a projected point-of-conception-to-point-of-completion time of two to two-and-a-half years, this option, too, was ruled out. Seven architecture firms were invited by the university to present solutions to this difficult problem. Moody Moore Duncan Rattray Peters Searle Christie (MMDRPSC) was chosen, because it seemed to take the "most imaginative approach."

MMDRPSC proposed a low rise "groundscraper," a "blending" structure that would improve connections between various parts of the campus. As to the location of the groundscraper, "the concept evolved," in the words of James Christie, partner-in-charge, "as an informal system going up, over and around the existing buildings, utilizing the spaces between and above . . . ." *(Figures 181, 182)*

Figures 183, 184. Interior views of Centennial Hall's internal "street," showing the exposed floor-depth trusses and the stairs and escalators joining different levels.

How and where to support the new building? "We had two choices," says MMDRPSC partner Mike Rattray, "either punch down through the existing buildings, or go down over them onto the sidewalk." To disrupt the university schedule as little as possible, the firm opted for the latter, the concept of supporting the building on columns placed on the sidewalk, in front of the existing buildings.

Leaving aside the question of whether the sidewalks *could* be used in this way (they were eventually), the next problem was one of spans between possible supports, spans which ran to thirty-six metres (120 feet) in length. Because engineers recommended two-metre (six-and-one-half-foot) deep trusses, too deep to place in a dropped ceiling without wasting a great deal of space, it was eventually decided to use full-storey trusses. This meant that one floor could be rested on the top chord of the truss, and another hung from the bottom chord, necessitating trusses only every other floor. Thus, two basic engineering concepts, the "stilt concept" and the "full storey truss concept," underlay the complex and radical-looking building which MMDRPSC proposed

for this "little university on this little piece of ground."

Officially opened in September 1972, Centennial Hall, as the new structure has been named, has vastly improved connections between various parts of the campus. Based on an analogy to automobile circulation, where roads vary according to the flow and speed of traffic, a spacious interior pedestrian "street" was created on a north-south axis running through the heart of the new structure and, consequently, the campus as well. In addition to its horizontal function, this "street" has a vertical component: a set of escalators connecting the four floors of the new building in an uninterrupted straight line. Large courtyards are cut out of the building along this spine of escalators, and generous windows allow views out and light in. A trip through this "street" at the heart of the building, which provides access to the rest of the university, reveals overhead a collage of ducts, pipes, exposed three-metre-deep (ten-foot) trusses, interior and exterior spaces, and a series of department store-like exhibits of light, colour and form. *(Figures 183, 184)*

Figures 185, 186. University of Winnipeg, Centennial Hall, the western edge of the site. Moody Moore et al., Architects.

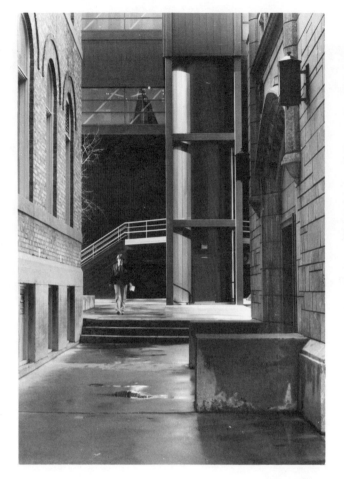

From the outside, futuristic notions of urban design seem to have been combined with the most matter-of-fact and traditional concepts of buildings on streets, sidewalks and courtyards. Clad in dark bronze-finished steel panels, the new building juts out over the sidewalk, beginning at the third storey on one side, and the fourth storey on the other. The walls of Centennial Hall are simply perpendicular to the street, continuing the lines established by the older buildings. Equally important, the new building carefully reinforces the central courtyard. *(Figures 185, 186, 187, 188, 189)*

The Portage Avenue facade of the University of Winnipeg, *the* image of the university to the rest of the city, is considerably strengthened by the addition of Centennial Hall. The grey slate roof of Wesley Hall is pointed up by the dark colour of the new metal building. The symmetrical facade of Wesley Hall, with its twin towers and sloping roof in between, is echoed in the more modern but similarly-formed front of Centennial Hall. Bryce Hall, a small, previously insignificant limestone building, now stands out against a dark metal background. Now more than ever before, the University of Winnipeg presents a handsome, balanced composition of new and old to the rest of the city.

Figure 187. View of Centennial Hall, framed by Wesley and Bryce Halls.

Figure 188. The new building reinforces the existing courtyard.

Figure 189. University of Winnipeg, the Portage Avenue facade — a balance between new and old. Moody Moore et al., Architects.

Citadel Theatre, Edmonton

The site proposed for the Citadel Theatre in downtown Edmonton was in some ways no less difficult than that proposed for Centennial Hall. Not only was the Edmonton site small, but there was an existing garage on its western edge. To complicate matters further, Edmonton's City Planners had proposed a street-level nine-metre-wide (thirty-foot) public walkway to cut through the centre of the site and, eventually, through the theatre itself.

Of five architecture firms invited to submit proposals for the site, the Toronto firm of Diamond and Myers, in association with the Edmonton architect R. L. Wilkin, was chosen for the job. Rather than finding the dimensions and conditions of the site restrictive or daunting, architect Barton Myers saw them as "challenging." "Constraints," he explains, "often become the generators of ideas."

One of the more difficult aspects of theatre design is the strict segregation required between the public "front of house" functions, and the private, production-related functions of the "back of house." Responding not only to this particular characteristic of theatres, but also to the specific nature of the Citadel site in Edmonton, Myers and his associates utilized the proposed walkway as a natural dividing line through the theatre, locating "front of house" functions on one side of it, and "back of house" functions on the other. *(Figures 190, 191)*

Figure 190. Citadel Theatre, Edmonton, the "transparent" west face, corresponding to the "front of house" functions. Diamond and Myers, in association with R.L. Wilkin, Architects; Barton Myers, partner-in-charge.

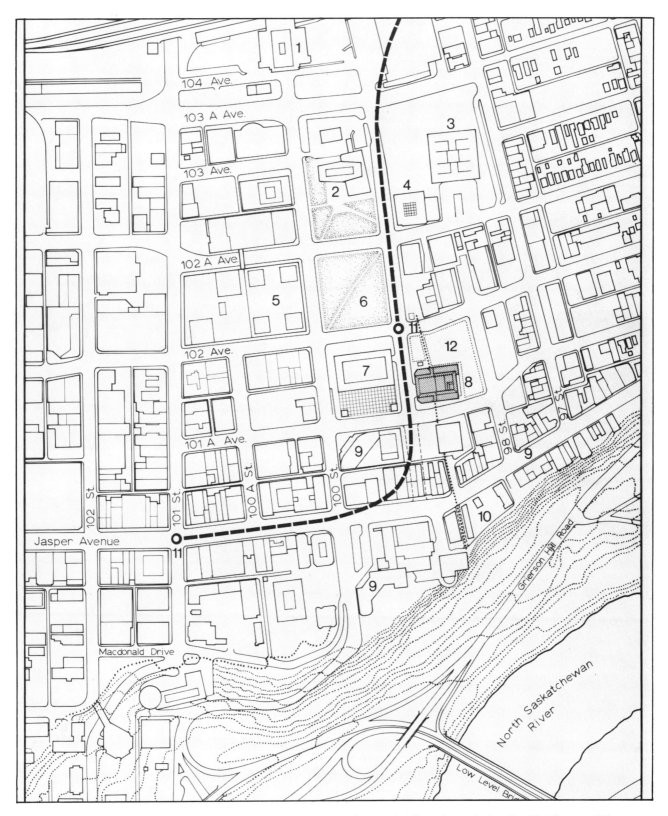

Figure 191. Site plan of the Citadel Theatre, Edmonton.

Figure 192. The walkway, inside the Citadel Theatre complex,
from which all three of the complex's theatres are reached.

Figure 193. The comparatively "opaque" east face of the Citadel Theatre, the "back of house." Barton Myers, partner-in-charge.

Opening in 1976, the concept underlying the building's design was that, proceeding along the street-level walkway, one would be able to get a sense of the overall feeling of the theatre, and the location of its constituent parts. Thus, all three of the building's theatres, the Shoctor Theatre, which is the largest, and the Rice and Zeidler theatres, are entered directly from the walkway: the lobby of the Rice Theatre is down a few steps; the Zeidler Theatre is on the same level as the walkway; and the Shoctor Theatre can be reached via a wide, elegant stairway which begins at the walkway. The impact of the Shoctor Theatre on the walkway is especially strong: the stepped underside of that theatre's floor forms the gently terraced ceiling of the walkway itself. *(Figure 192)*

Other openings in the walls of the walkway reveal the Citadel's various public facilities, including its bar, restaurant, box offices and a rather emphatically-lit coat check. The materials of the space are hard and tough: brick walls, tile floor, and concrete ceiling. Appropriately, the walkway seems more an extension of the outside sidewalk than a separate, isolated place.

From the outside, the distinction between "front of house" and "back of house," becomes more evident through the thoughtful and consistent handling of materials. The public "front of house" functions on one side of the walkway are expressed in terms of *transparency*: the front of the building is essentially all glass, a curtain wall. By contrast, those of the private "back of house" are expressed in terms of *opacity*: the back of the theatre is mostly solid brick, its openings punched out only where necessary. *(Figure 193)*

Figure 194. Interior of a rehearsal hall, Citadel Theatre.

Myers' predisposition towards juxtaposing "opposites," whether "metaphysical," in his words, "or purely design devices," is evidenced not only by the transparent/opaque dichotomy of the exterior, but also by equally clear oppositions between front and back created throughout the interior of the building. Towards this end, details and finishes are chosen with extreme care and skill.

With its grey-carpeted floors, and concrete block walls outlined by a poured concrete frame, the "back of house" ranges in feeling from a neutral tone for the office and administrative areas, to the straightforward industrial character of the workshops and rehearsal halls. *(Figure 194)*

Front of house functions, epitomized by the glass-wrapped Shoctor Lobby at the front of the building, are much more plush, colourful and generally more "decorated." The red colour of the Medicine Hat brick, used on the exterior and interior, is echoed in the front of house choice of rust-red carpet and red clay tile floors, burgundy-coloured fabric on the theatre seats, and redwood walls in the Shoctor and Zeidler theatres. While metal window-wall frames have also been enamelled a similar rust-red, other metal fittings, such as stair railings, are brass, creating thin lines and small spots of flash and brilliance within the multi-level, free-flowing space of the central Shoctor Lobby. *(Figures 195, 196, 197)*

Figures 195, 196. Citadel Theatre complex, the lobby and the interior of the Schocter Theatre — "front of house" is plush, colourful and more decorated. Barton Myers, partner-in-charge.

Figure 197. The lobby at night.

Figure 198. Citadel Theatre. Glass arcade on 101A Avenue, one of three arcaded sides of the building.

Viewed from nearby Sir Winston Churchill Square, the squat, red brick theatre with its glass front stands out amidst a surrounding environment of recent, pre-cast concrete buildings which are generally the same on all four sides. The fact that the building does not blend in with its recent neighbors, however, is here a good thing. The front/back dichotomy which accounts for the internal order of the Citadel, also makes sense when one looks at the theatre within a larger urban context. The glass-wrapped front of the building faces onto 99th Street, one of Edmonton's major streets, upon which sits not only the nearby Winston Churchill Square, but also the city's main post office, police headquarters, and the Edmonton Art Gallery. The service-oriented, predominantly-opaque back of the building faces onto the decidedly less important 98th Street.

In deference to surrounding streets, and in hope of re-establishing the traditional, pre-eminent image of streets as volumes — enclosed and defined by the parallel walls of buildings on both sides — the bulk of the Citadel is pushed right up to the sidewalk on all four sides. A glass arcade extends protectively over the sidewalk on three sides of the building. This arcade system, explains Barton Myers, "could easily be incorporated in(to) our cities to make the sidewalk experience less gruesome during inclement weather." *(Figure 198)*

As in Winnipeg's Centennial Hall, an endorsement of traditional and matter-of-fact patterns of urban design has not prevented the designer from tapping the exciting and liberating realm of forms, materials and spaces that remain a positive legacy of the birth of the modern movement. In order to explain the building, Myers refers to his original mandate, that of creating a "warm and theatrical place." Through the juxtaposition of old and new, traditional and modern, a spirit of warmth and theatre pervades not only the Citadel's interior, but also is conveyed through the building's glass face out onto a section of one of Edmonton's most important streets. Of future buildings, in cities across the country, Canadians should demand no less. *(Figure 199)*

Figure 199. The Citadel Theatre at night, a "warm and theatrical place." Diamond and Myers, in association with R.L. Wilkin, Architects; Barton Myers, partner-in-charge.

VII Beyond the Mainstream

Beyond the hope that a building will satisfy the use for which it has been commissioned, there is in all innovative architecture the larger strategy to influence some aspect of the future environment. With infill projects, the strategy is to consolidate low-rise city fabric, and to set a standard for the building outlines of neighbouring developments to follow. Buildings such as the Dufferin/ St. Clair Library (Baird/Sampson Associates, 1979), the Seagram Museum (Barton Myers Associates, 1983), the YMCA of Metropolitan Toronto (A.J. Diamond & Partners, 1984), Lux (Luc Laporte, 1985), and the Canadian Centre for Architecture (Peter Rose Associés, Architectes, 1988) represent new and diverse approaches to "infilling" the densely packed urban context. Issues fundamental to architectural design — formal composition, the detailing of facades and interiors — have gained significance as the sense of conflict with mainstream development fades from the written and built statements of the coun-try's most innovative architects. While the infill strategy has continued to be an important, even dominant approach for architects building within well-defined downtown areas, many of the most radical recent projects have been commissioned in the ever-expanding suburban periphery. Mississauga City Hall (Jones & Kirkland, Architects, 1987), the Pyrch Residence (Patkau Architects, 1984), the Harbourview Recreational Centre (IKOY Architects, 1982), Coquitlam's Town Centre Firehall and Training Centre (Henriquez & Partners, Architects, 1986), and the Lethbridge Construction (Melvin Charney, 1985) are all projects that address the sprawling and ambiguous condition of the suburban and exurban areas in which they are set. In the ongoing creation of new paradigms of development, these recent projects for the urban core and the urban fringe offer alternatively a vision of revived romanticism and the search for a clearly contemporary architectural expression.

Figure 200 Plan of the Dufferin/St. Clair Library (Baird/Sampson Associates, 1979).

Dufferin/St. Clair Library

This iconoclastic transformation of a public lending library in a predominantly Italian residential area of Toronto recovers classical characteristics that had been purged from the original 1920's building through a series of earlier renovations. The historically sensitive addition and modernist renovation combine to make a provocative statement on the language of architecture, a long-standing concern of this project's architects, George Baird and Barry Sampson.

Two new wings, lower in height than the existing building, have been added to house the library's growing collection of books, permitting the central building's high-ceilinged ground floor rooms to be restored for a variety of public uses. *(Figure 200)* The two new wings

project forward to the street line, strengthening the central portico and creating a shallow forecourt that graciously accommodates stairs and a ramp. The new ramp, a provision for the handicapped, subtly unbalances the symmetry of the front facade's composition. A new metal cornice structure carrying lighting unifies the new ensemble of the aggrandized main building with its stepped wings. *(Figure 201)*

Inside the renovated library, a character of almost-domestic cosiness has been created with the addition of a broad fireplace with fixed upholstered benches with bookshelves built into their backs. Although located just above ground level, the two new wings have an attic-like ambience as a consequence of the long and narrow pro-

Figure 201 Dufferin Street facade of the Dufferin/St. Clair Library.

Figure 202 Axonometric drawing showing the renovated library with its two new wing additions to the north and south.

Figure 203 South-facing facade of the Dufferin/St. Clair Library.

Figure 204 Detail photograph of the bay window in the south facade of the Dufferin/St. Clair Library.

portions of their low-ceilinged space, and the placement of bookstacks in a series of intimately scaled alcoves. The low height of the new wings' roofs leaves intact a row of clerestory windows that admit light into the north and south sides of the original library. *(Figure 202)*

Alterations to the existing building are applied in a visibly fragmentary way to the exterior of the building, as successive layers of ornament. The veneer of stairs and ramps has been integrated with a new rusticated concrete block base; this base serves as the foundation of the new wings, giving an appearance of consistency and mass to the ensemble. The exterior wall of the longer south wing shows most dramatically the complex, successive layering of materials: metal cornice, brick skin, concrete coping and base, window frame and bay, and eventually, the simple stucco shed addition that, as it recedes from the street, stands free of all ornament, a simple foreground to the partially revealed southern wall of the original building. *(Figures 203, 204)* Legible on this wall, which wraps around to integrate with the reinvigorated front facade of the library, are the outline, the successive drafts, and the denouement of an accomplished essay on the language of contemporary architecture.

Seagram Museum

With the Seagram tower in New York (Mies van der Rohe, 1959), the Joseph E. Seagram & Sons company embraced a corporate image of minimalism, consistency, and control that is characteristic of the work of its architect, a pioneer of the Modern movement and a leading exponent of Modernism in North America. Seeking to expand that image in the early 1980's, Chairman Charles Bronfman commissioned Barton Myers Associates (design architects of the Citadel Theatre, Chapter 5) to design a corporate museum on the site of the nineteenth-century Seagram distillery at Waterloo, Ontario.

Unlike the Platonically pure design of the company's New York headquarters, the Museum makes use of mundane elements of the industrial complex, most notably the barrel storage warehouse that occupies the site's major frontage at the corner of Caroline and Erb Streets. As both major frontages were usurped by the retained warehouse, and the southern edge of the site was bordered by a larger, active distillery building, the new part of the Museum occupies a low-profile area between the two. The renovated barrel warehouse is the entrance to the new Museum, accommodating a restaurant and specialty shop. An arrival court has been created by the removal of a central portion of the heavy timber racks; the remaining racks extend up an impressive five levels to form the defining framework of the skylit court. *(Figures 205, 206)*

As a consequence of its unassuming fit between existing structures, the building is experienced as a sequence of interdependent interior spaces rather than as an object symbolizing an external corporate image. *(Figure 207)* Within its skylit steel frame, the Museum contains four small steel pavilions. The first level of the pavilions is devoted to a sequence of exhibition themes and media; the upper level houses the company archives and Museum offices. A decked-over creek which was the original source of the distilleries makes its presence felt in the court as a diagonal threshold paved in slate. A steel-framed tower — designed to house a particularly tall still — and the rear corner of one of the pavilions project out

Figure 205 Site plan of the Seagram Museum. 1 Plant Offices 2 New Gate House 3 Boiler Plant 4 Museum Arrival Courtyard 5 Renovated Warehouse 6 Museum and Archives 7 Existing Production Building 8 Existing Fermenting Building 9 Existing Bottling Building.

Figure 206 A liquor store (seen to the left), restaurant (centre), and coatroom are accommodated in the renovated barrel storage warehouse. Wood removed from the rack storage structure to create a skylit entry court was refinished for use in the new Museum, which adjoins the warehouse.

Figure 207 Looking from the skylit court of the new Seagram Museum towards the renovated barrel storage warehouse.

of the west wall of the building, propelled by the geometry of the exhibit hall plan. *(Figure 208)*

Exterior walls of the Museum are buff brick with paired bands of red brick, in reference to the buff warehouse foreground and red bottling building background. Spacing of the red brick bands approximates the five levels of windows in the old warehouse, while the lower and upper lines of the Museum roof relate back to the east facade of the bottling building. Two metal clad "dormers" housing mechanical equipment and three large windows are the sole, utilitarian improvisations within the conciliatory composition of the Museum's principle new exterior wall. *(Figure 209)* Although it evinces a degree of restraint that might be compared to that of the New York headquarters building, the Seagram Museum does so in the distinctively composite vocabulary of its architect, Barton Myers.

Figure 208 View of the front door of the Seagram Museum; the still tower is seen to the right. In the foreground, a pyramid of barrels provides both a turn-around for buses and a marker for the unassuming entrance.

Figure 209 Overview of the Seagram Museum (Barton Myers Associates, 1983) showing the renovated barrel storage warehouse in the foreground of the new Museum structure.

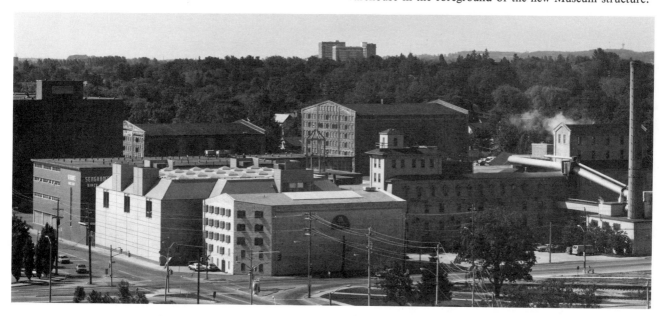

Metropolitan Central YMCA

With comparable understatement to the previous projects, but with a greater emphasis on the formal expression of its functional components, A.J. Diamond & Partners designed the Metropolitan Central YMCA as a series of five structurally distinct buildings linked into a larger aggregate on an odd-shaped downtown site. *(Figures 210, 211)*

Facing Grosvenor Street, a wing of racquet courts and exercise rooms steps forward, creating a forecourt between the Y and a neighbouring fire hall. The Y is entered through a building between, and set back from,

the courts and fire station. Contained in the set-back building is a cylindrical Rotunda that holds a childrens' swimming pool at the ground level and an auditorium above. *(Figure 212)* Literally and figuratively the hinge about which the other programme components rotate, the Rotunda is clad in light-coloured reconstituted stone like other upper-level elements of the Y, thereby lifting it out of the mass of the brick entry building in which it sits. From Grosvenor, the cylindrical mass of the Rotunda is visible behind another smaller cylindrical form, also contained in the entry building but appearing

Figure 211 Roof plan, Central YMCA.

Figure 212 Partial view of the Rotunda at the second floor level, showing public walkway leading past the gymnasium to the left and the swimming pool, visible through windows seen through the doorway to the right.

Figure 210 Overview of the Metropolitan Central YMCA (A.J. Diamond & Partners, 1984). The firehall is seen in the foreground to the right.

to emerge out of its mass; this smaller cylinder houses the stair that leads to a second floor public passageway that traverses the site from Grosvenor to Breadalbane Street. Two long-span buildings, rectangular in shape, abut the north and west faces of the entry building. The gymnasium and its roof-top running track, to the west of the entry building, form a higher, more massive volume crested by a shallow, V-shaped cutout parapet wall. *(Figure 213)* The pool wing, to the north of the entry

Figure 213 The gymnasium wing of the Central YMCA, viewed from the west; the cut-out parapet wall along the roof-top running track is seen upper left.

Figure 214 The skylit vaulted ceiling of the YMCA pool recalls the Roman Thermae, a place of sport and an urban institution.

Figure 215 Entrance to the Central YMCA from Breadalbane Street. To the right, the vaulted pool, to the left, the administration.

building, has a distinctive vaulted roof, punctuated by a pattern of small domed skylights. *(Figure 214)* The fifth building, housing a daycare and administrative offices, is cubic in volume with a pronounced frame asserting its concrete structure. The merging of the administration building's facade with that of the pool creates a unified curve of glass block, signalling entrance to the public passage-way from Breadalbane Street. *(Figure 215)*

The Central YMCA maintains a careful balance of material solidity and formal inventiveness in its masonry-clad ensemble: the office wing, the pool, the gym, the entry building with its two cylinders, and the wing of racquet courts enjoy a studied equilibrium that arises in equal parts out of the jig-saw configuration of the site and the projection of programme components into articulate building forms.

Lux

Lux is a transformation of a dilapidated industrial building into a commercial complex that is effectively a new indoor public space in Montreal's St. Laurent Street area. The area itself is remarkable for its appropriation by a number of unaffiliated entrepreneurs, along the lines of European urban centres — or indeed Canadian urban areas of a bygone era — where neighbourhood restaurateurs, store-owners, and self-styled impresarios have generated lively downtown public spaces without trading up to large-scale "revitalization" by mammoth development companies.

Behind the barely altered front facade of the original building (a sign made of oversize, jumbled, three-dimensional letters made of lights and spelling LUX is the only external indication of what is to come), portions of floors have been removed to create a cylindrical open space. *(Figure 216)* Two steel stairs spiral up along the perimeter of this cylinder under a frosted glass dome. A

Figure 216 The barely altered St. Laurent facade of Lux (Luc Laporte, 1985).

Figure 217 A cylindrical space has been created at the centre of the former industrial/commercial building; skylighting and spiralling stairs give a peripatetic character to the café.

collar of mirrors rings the circular third floor opening, reflecting jumbled views of the sky and surrounding buildings. The image of buildings is in fact intensified by the installation of mirrors outside the dome: these multiply the apparent density of the immediate context by reflecting neighbouring buildings and transmitting their shadowy outlines through the frosted panes of the dome. *(Figures 217, 218)*

Accomodating a café on the ground floor, the cylinder is ringed by an assortment of retail uses, none of which has the expected demising walls, doors, or signage typical of commercial malls. As if lifted from a 1940's film set or a Parisian café, a zinc bar with textured glass and steel light fixtures and shelves crosses the entire width of the back wall of the building. To either side of the cylindrical space, new steel mezzanines have

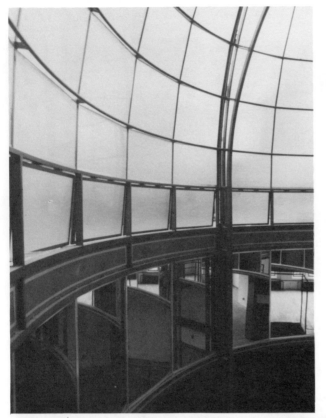

been added for open magazine stands. *(Figure 219)* To either side of the St. Laurent Street entrance are unpretentious small stores selling food and wine; shelving, counters, and lights are of the same design as in other parts of the project: steel painted a glossy Paris-subway-green, textured glass, simple incandescent lighting. A hybrid of the literary café and the North American shopping mews, Lux presents an arresting alternative to the formulaic development with its predictable atrium.

Figure 218 Outside the dome of the skylight, mirrors multiply the apparent density of the immediate context by reflecting neighbouring buildings and transmitting their shadowy outlines through the frosted panes of glass.

Figure 219 New steel split-level magazine stands flank the cylindrical central space: both the programme of functions and the glossy Paris-subway-green finishes evoke the atmosphere of the European literary café with its simultaneously commerical and intellectual, public life.

The Canadian Centre for Architecture

The design of the Canadian Centre for Architecture represents a rapprochment of modern and classical tendencies in architecture. For client/consulting architect Phyllis Lambert, once the Director of Planning for the Seagram tower (Mies van der Rohe, 1959) in New York and the design architect of the Miesian Saidye Bronfman Centre in Montreal, the historically referential renovation and expansion of a downtown Montreal landmark reflects the impact of a quarter century of collecting and work in preservation. Peter Rose, whose early work reflects the influence of his former teacher and well-known revivalist of historical styles, Charles Moore, has conversely moved away from the ironic classical references of the St. Sauveur resort (see Pavilion '70, Chapter 5), and closer to an austere, but richly finished architecture evocative of the early modernist work of Erik Gunnar Asplund or Adolf Loos.

The CCA is of critical importance to contemporary architects, at least as much for cultural as for architectural reasons. With a collection of 100,000 books, draw-

Figure 220 Axonometric view of the building for the Canadian Centre for Architecture (Peter Rose, Architect; Phyllis Lambert, Consulting Architect, 1988).

Figure 221 The centrepiece Shaughnessy Mansion (William T. Thomas, 1875), prior to construction of the new CCA.

Plan général/General plan

Figure 222 Plan of the CCA building (Dorchester Boulevard is seen running along the top edge of the plan): 1 Entrance 2 Exhibition galleries 3 Bookstore 4 Great Hall 5 Library reading room 6 Rare documents cabinet 7 Scholars' offices 8 Reception rooms 9 Restaurant 10 Auditorium 11 Public park.

Figure 223 Aerial view of the site model showing Dorchester Boulevard facade of the CCA: the Shaughnessy Mansion is flanked by the Auditorium to the left and the research wing to the right.

ings, and photographs, the rapidly expanding Centre will grow to rival the Public Archives of Canada's architectural collection, which currently holds the nation's most extensive design record with a collection of some 250,000 items.

The facility in which the Centre is housed is a new greystone building organized in a U-Shape around an existing Victorian mansion known as the Shaughnessy House. *(Figure 220)* Actually a pair of semi-detached houses, this remnant of Montreal's great industrial prosperity is named after the third owner of the east house, railroad magnate Thomas G. Shaughnessy. The building, which was the lone survivor of a grand boulevard of stately homes, was saved from demolition in 1973 when it was purchased by Phyllis Lambert. *(Figure 221)*

The new building surrounds the old on three sides, and is linked centrally to it by means of a narrow, skylit passage. *(Figure 222)* The entrance to the Centre has been redirected to the north into the new institutional-scale building, with the centrepiece Mansion and its new flanking wings standing symbolically like three reconstituted mansions along fast-paced Dorchester Boulevard. *(Figure 223)*

The new Centre places functions accessible to outsiders on its "piano nobile," or second floor: 30,000 square feet of exhibition galleries, the library reading room, and a bookstore occupy the massive north wing;

Figure 224 Aerial view of the site model facing south. Reception rooms and restaurant replace the dining room and salons of the former Mansion, while new wing to the north houses a ground-level curatorial facility and upper level exhibition and research spaces.

rare documents and scholars' offices occupy the east wing flanking Dorchester. A 250-seat auditorium constitutes the west wing, and reception and a restaurant replace the dining room and salons of the former Mansion. A rusticated base clads what is actually the ground floor, which functions as a curatorial level equipped with offices, archival and shipping facilities. *(Figure 224)*

By maintaining a consistently lower new wall, and by integrating the bases of the new and former buildings, architects Rose and Lambert have emphasized the mass and horizontal length of the ensemble. Few windows interrupt the greystone surface at the second level, which is the tallest in height. This emphasis on the mass and the length of the new walls offsets the Victorian Mansion, with its regular pattern of skinny windows, narrow projecting bays and shallow mansard expressing the tall, upright character of the mid-nineteenth century Neo-Gothic style.

Mississauga City Hall

Although it is located in the sparsely developed vicinity of an existing shopping centre and a handful of mid-rise suburban office towers, Jones & Kirkland Architects' competition-winning design for a new city hall transplants many of the contextualist attitudes of the infill genre to the hitherto centre-less bedroom community of Mississauga. The City Hall represents a stong resistance to the vacancy of its surrounding context. Following the spirit of the competition brief prepared by Baird/Sampson Associates, the architects designed a City Hall which gathers the building functions at the north end of a public square that is defined on its eastern and western edges by monumentally scaled pedestrian arcades. *(Figure 225)*

The arcades end at the southern end of the site, at Burnhamthorpe Road, and are terminated by pavilions that neatly conceal ramps down to an underground parking garage. *(Figure 226)* Dominating the composition of building forms at the north edge of the central square is an enormous gabled building clad in buff brick. At once vernacular (a super-scale suburban farmhouse in the foreground of its sheds and silo) and classical (the pediment symbolizing its role as a public institution), the

Figure 225 Aerial view, Mississauga Civic Centre (Jones & Kirkland, 1987).

GROUND FLOOR PLAN

Figure 226 Ground floor plan, Mississauga City Hall.

Figure 227 North-south section through the Civic Centre, taken through the Great Hall and showing the clock tower and office building in the background.

SECTION B-B

gabled building commands the vast width of the site. Assembled behind the gabled building are five interconnected buildings of distinctly individual form; these emerge out of a common plinth that accommodates a drop of elevation across the length of the site as it descends toward Lake Ontario. *(Figure 227)* Suggestive of a work of sculpture in progress, the fragmentary forms of the pyramidal roof of the grand hall, the drum of the council chamber, the tapering clock tower and the stepped office tower stand behind the broad gable of the front building. Both the composite mass and the sober, unadorned style of the building result from a studied combination of architectural allusions.

Inside the City Hall, the interior detailing of the different building components lends material as well as formal autonomy. Sensual, dark green Italian marble banded with black granite clad the walls of the skylit Great Hall, and a richly polished, ochre-coloured stone gridded in black granite covers the floor. *(Figures 228, 229)* Ringing the cylindrical Council Chamber is a row of doubled columns, a reference to the colonnade of Perrault, designed for the east front of the Louvre in 1665 and famous in art history as a definitive statement of French classical architecture. *(Figure 230)* In the office tower, open office landscape has been eschewed in favour of ordered and defined workspace. As such,

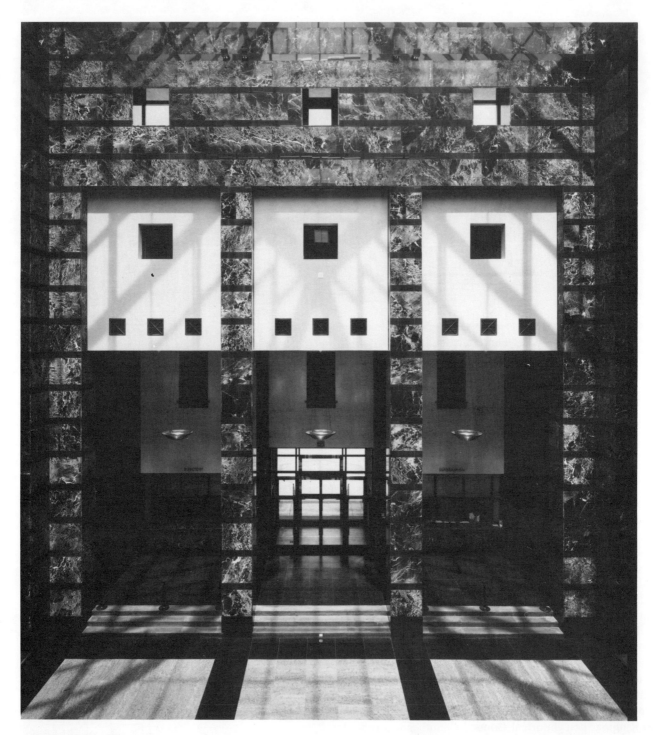

Mississauga's City Hall is a demonstration of a more structured, and more considered suburban architecture of the future. Its impact on local developers remains to be tested; the importance of its polemic for architects practising in exurban areas across Canada has already been profound.

Figure 228 Inside the Great Hall, looking north.

Figure 229 Inside the Great Hall, looking through the arched opening towards the Conservatory with its view south to Lake Ontario.

Figure 230 Inside the Council Chamber; the names of townships amalgamated to form Mississauga decorate the entablature.

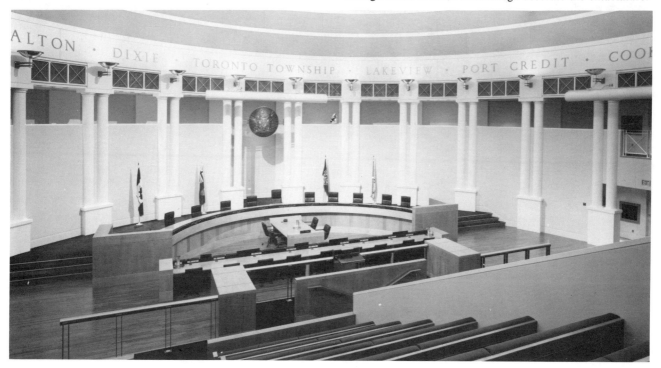

The Pyrch Residence

Built on an irregular, rocky site in a larger subdivision on the outskirts of Victoria, B.C., the Pyrch house is a spare and lyrical assembly of volumes. *(Figure 231)* The living room, with its chiselled copper roof evoking a miniature château, steps forward of the splayed, lower wings, dignifying the front of the house, notwithstanding its inevitable two-car garage. *(Figure 232)*

The siting of the house shuns the neighbouring subdivision, focusing inwardly on an existing rock terrace and a distant view of the ocean. *(Figure 233)* Respecting what the Patkaus felt was a predilection for the abstract

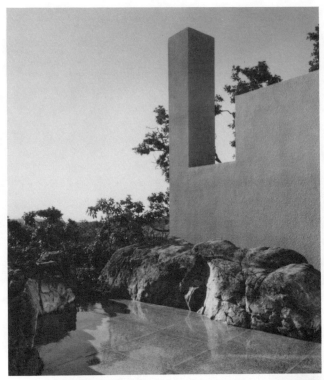

Figure 231 A spare and lyrical interpretation of a baronial manor, the Pyrch residence in Victoria, B.C. (Patkau Architects, 1984) focuses on an existing rock terrace and a distant view of the ocean, rather than addressing the houses in its suburban context.

Figure 232 The front of the house reveals little of the splayed, lower wings beyond, making its presence on the street extraordinarily understated.

on the part of their art-collecting clients, the architects composed the house in a series of discrete, elemental gestures. The use of a concealed flashing at the top of the wall, for instance, eliminates the customary edge that borders stucco finish, and helps to define the stucco volumes against the sky.

Pencil-proportioned chimneys pull out from the ends of the two wings — one for living spaces, the other shorter one for a master bedroom suite — framing the rock terrace. *(Figure 234)* Skylights are used to further sculpt the elemental, fortress-like spaces: a long narrow rectangular skylight stretches along the edge of the long and narrow

Figure 233 Site plan, the Pyrch residence.

Figure 234 Slender chimneys mark the ends of the two wings — to the right, a wing of living spaces terminated in a breakfast room; to the left, a shorter master bedroom wing.

Figure 235 Building section through living room (above); "un-folded" building section (below); sectional drawings show extensive millwork casings surrounding windows.

Figure 236 View through living room window showing the use of glossily finished millwork casing around windows to bounce the light.

dining room; a trapedzoidal skylight lends complexity to the wedge-shaped breakfast room. Windows are framed by deep millwork casings that have been painted with a high-gloss finish to bounce light and assert their diverse forms.*(Figure 235, 236)*

The design of the Pyrch residence counters the repetitive suburban model with a highly individualized response to the absence of urban density. Not only does the house make its own idiosyncratic adjustments to the landscape, it proposes a landscape — albeit an abstract one — of architectural forms that evoke the rugged isolation of grand historical residences.

Harbourview Recreational Centre

Located on the outskirts of Winnipeg in the midst of industrial and undeveloped lands is Harbourview, a
municipal recreation complex. Harbourview is a picturesque village of buildings that compartmentalize various
aspects of a sport-oriented programme: a golfers' pro
shop, locker rooms, restaurant, and lookout tower.
(Figure 237) These components are linked into a larger
ensemble by a covered walkway. *(Figure 238)*

Belying its quaint seaside village image, Harbourview's wood structure is a pre-manufactured house truss
system. In the words of its designer, Ron Keenberg,
"what we are striving for is machine craftsmanship, not
handcraft. We try to use off-the-shelf components
wherever possible. Craftsmanship comes from
assembly."

The assembly, technically as well as formally, creates
the impression of a past that has been incompletely
retrieved. The repetitive pairs of timber light standards
along the dock conjure up the rustic images of power or
telegraph links — images historically poignant in the
prairie countryside — but their toy-railroad scale and visible finity make clear that this is a fragmentary, totemic
image, not to be taken at face value. In the same way,
the wood clapboard and heavy timbers conjure up the
image of a farm, but the dark glass of the windows, the
dark finishes on sash and muntin bars make the windows

Figure 238 Looking under the walkway towards the restaurant
wing.

Figure 237 View of Harbourview (IKOY Architects, 1982) from
the man-made lake.

Figure 239 Wood clapboard and heavy timber conjure up the image of a farm, but the windows' dark glass and frames make the windows look empty, as if the buildings had been abandoned.

Figure 240 Inside, smooth white walls and unpainted pre-fab wood trusses reverse the outer image of the building: the display of structural and electrical components makes the buildings appear modern, in process of construction.

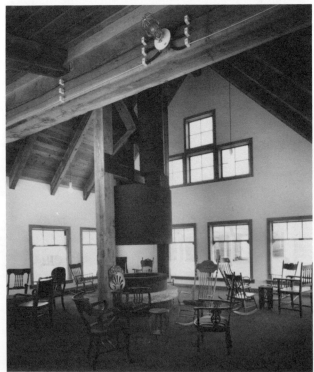

look empty, as if the buildings had been abandoned. *(Figure 239)* Inside, smooth white walls, the unpainted pre-fab wood trusses and wood-framed windows reverse the illusion: we are in a modern space, in process of construction. *(Figure 240)* If Harbourview, as one observer commented, "evokes a history the project has never known," it also points toward a wittily ironic future for architectural symbolism and technology.

Coquitlam Town Centre Firehall and Training Centre

Designed like Mississauga City Hall as the heraldic institution of a yet-to-be-developed town ensemble, the Coquitlam Firehall achieves instant complexity through a combination of evocative elements. *(Figure 241)* A large stepped-roof garage of apparatus bays, out of which thrusts a hose-drying tower, is pried away from a structure holding sleeping and recreational rooms for the firemen. *(Figures 242, 243)* Holding these two facilities apart is a skylit wedge-shaped building carrying stairs and crowned with a cone-topped cylindrical communications tower. Bulging out of the east wall of the dormitory building are projecting lounge spaces; the outer carved

GROUND FLOOR PLAN

Figure 241 Ground Floor Plan, Coquitlam Town Centre Firehall and Training Centre (Henriquez & Partners, Architects, 1986) 1 Hosedrying tower 2 Clean room 3 Workshop 4 Projection room 5 Storage 6 Training classroom 7 Apparatus bays 8 Janitor 9 Office 10 Alarm room 11 Kitchen 12 Lounge 13 Entry 14 Dining 15 Assistant fire chief 16 Office 17 Fire chief 18 Meeting room 19 Lobby 20 Secretaries 21 Fire prevention work area 22 Fire prevention officer 23 Conference 24 Coffee 25 Lounge 26 Library 27 Flagpole.

Figure 242 View from Training Tower towards west side of the Firehall.

Figure 243 South elevation showing stepped profile of the apparatus bays.

Figure 244 East elevation with its projecting lounge space; visible beyond is the cone-topped cylindrical communications tower.

Figure 245 The training tower: an example of the international evolution in architectural design that includes allusion to the historical period of Modernism and its spinoff, the Constructivist movement.

surface carries a flag that aligns with a paved circular walk. *(Figure 244)* Tangential to this circular walk, but pulled away from the main body of the Firehall is a wing of administrative offices. The splayed geometries of the component buildings suggests a centrifugal pattern, a familiar Constructivist gesture. *(Figure 245)*

Architect Richard Henriquez claims that the vacancy of the site inspired the imploded composition of the building. For him, the Firehall is a facility that has "fragmented and evolved from a base building through a series of 'growth' stages . . . This evolution of elements begins to suggest a simulated past attempting to integrate with a simulated future." Disturbing the predictable structural order of the building, the Firehall's communications room's cylindrical shape implies a firmly-founded tower, but in fact overhangs the gap between dorm and garage. *(Figure 246)*

Responsible for the more static Gaslight Square (see Chapter 5), Henriquez is both responding to the natural incomprehensibility of an undeveloped suburban site, and advancing his own interest in sculpture and assembly. Coquitlam's Firehall thus reflects the international evolution in architectural design — an evolution that now includes allusion to the historical period of Modernism and its spinoff movements like Constructivism — and the personal evolution of the architect as an artist.

Figure 246 The communications room's cylindrical shape and conical roof imply a firmly-founded tower, but in fact overhang the gap between dorm and garage, disturbing the predictable structural order of the building.

The Lethbridge Construction

Since carrying out the radical Corridart project (see Chapter 3) in Montreal, Melvin Charney has drawn for publication and built for art galleries in North America and Europe a number of conceptual projects that expand the way architects and artists look at their immediate environment. His constructions out of simple lumber are of great significance for the ongoing development of architectural thought as it pertains to an understanding of vernacular culture.

Invited in 1982 by Joan Stebbins to construct an "outdoor sculpture" for the Southern Alberta Art Gallery in Lethbridge, Alberta, Melvin Charney began by scrutinizing, photographing, and drawing the city and its surrounding prairie. His initial dismay at the sparseness of the built fabric gradually yielded, as, like a novelist, he recorded his evolving observations:

> I am distressed on arrival to find myself in an empty place, feeling betrayed by a sense of void . . . Here is a vestige of America as that open continent which received the first settlers. Here, then the drama of building in an original "void", bereft of history . . .
>
> It is this emptiness which exposes the historical features of the place . . . the so-called "false" fronts of buildings in the older parts of Lethbridge relate more to the real walls of the street as a defined place than to the often modest and "false" buildings which support them.

Disappointed by the superficiality of the sparsely built-up context of the Museum for which he had been originally asked to design an outdoor installation, Charney then turned to his own sketchbook to discover the substance behind prairie architecture. The "all-too-wide" streets, promoting passage through rather than settlement; the farm houses that "look as if they are the tops of buildings along the streets of an invisible city buried beneath the prairie"; the grain silos; the abandoned coal mineshaft; the railway viaduct: these disparate, heroic fragments were drawn, analyzed, and ultimately synthesized in the unbuilt Lethbridge Construction. *(Figures 247, 248, 249)*

Figure 247 "St. Anne's in Retlaw . . . Forgotten Cities," one of a series of drawings recording the architect's impressions of the disparate fragments of the Prairie townscape.

Figure 248 "Alberta Wheat Pool elevators as prairie houses," notebook sketch for a Lethbridge Construction (Melvin Charney, 1985).

Sited hypothetically at the west end of Fourth Avenue South, the heavy timber monument extends the Avenue onto a new trestle over a steep cliff. The bridge ends in mid-air at the alignment of the Oldman River below. Straddling the bridge on the brink of the coulee is a reconstructed grain elevator; a wood walkway bisects the upper shed of the elevator, perpendicular to the fragmentary trestle below. Inside, an elevator connects the two levels, allowing views out over "The Point," the now degenerate area of Lethbridge for which the construction is proposed. In Charney's terms, it would provide "a view of the libido of the city at work." *(Figures 250, 251)*

The purpose of Charney's proposal is to synthesize an image of his interpretation of the place. The result of the architect's analysis of Lethbridge as a representative prairie city is metaphor, the unexpected combination of fragmentary monuments that reveal the nature of the unfinished town fabric. And as in poetry, metaphor in architecture has the power to influence and enlarge the way we read the world around us.

Figure 249 Architect's photograph of a derelict coalmine shaft straddling the railway viaduct across the Oldman River coulee.

Figure 250 Notebook sketch studying the location of the Lethbridge Construction in relation to the derelict coalmine shaft, the coulee, and the town of Lethbridge.

Figure 251 "A Lethbridge Construction, No. 2": the unexpected combination of fragmentary monuments that reveal the nature of the unfinished Prairie town fabric.

Photography Credits

Arnott Rogers Batten Ltd., 83

Canada Museums Construction Corporation Inc., 16, 17, 18, 22, 25

Courtesy the Canadian Centre for Architecture, 220, 222

Cawker, Bernstein*, 5, 41, 43, 44, 45, 56, 58, 65, 67, 68, 69, 82, 84, 85, 86, 87, 92, 98, 102, 113, 127, 130, 131, 136, 140, 141, 142, 143, 156, 157, 158, 159, 160, 161, 168, 169, 170, 171, 172, 173, 176, 178, 184, 185, 186, 187, 188, 189, 190, 193, 198

Copyright Melvin Charney, 76, 79, 80, 81, 247, 248, 249, 250

Copyright Melvin Charney, courtesy the Canadian Centre for Architecture, 251

Courtesy Archives Nationales, 70, 71, 72, 73, 74, 75

Fraser Day, courtesy of National Gallery of Canada, 15, 23, 30, 32

Norman Cadorette, 119, 120

Eric Dandelin, 216, 217, 218, 219

James Dow, 231, 232, 233, 234, 236

Copyright Steven Evans, 214, 225, 228, 229, 230, front cover

Foto Blohm & Assoc., Ltd., 6, 7, 8, 9, 10, 11, 12

Graham French, 164

John Fulker, 132, 133, 134, 135, 137, 138, 194

Elizabeth Guilford, 46, 47, 48

Norman Hotson, 66

Timothy Hursley, c/o The Arkansaws Office, 206, 207, 208, 209, back cover

Jan Hughes, 95, 96, 97

Balthazar Korab, courtesy of I.M. Pei & Partners, 125

Copyright Phyllis Lambert/Richard Pare, courtesy the Canadian Centre for Architecture, 221

Lenscape Incorporated, 210

Marc Lullier, 118

Copyright Peter MacCallum, 204

Miller Services/H. Armstrong Roberts, 1

Miller Services/National Film Board, 2

NFB Photothèque ONF/Ted Grant, 3

Courtesy National Capital Commission, 51, 52, 53, 54

National Gallery of Canada, 24, 27, 28

Courtesy North Shore Archives, 129

Panda Associates, 60, 114

Courtesy I.M. Pei & Partners, 123, 124

Copyright Retoria: Y. Futagawa & Associates Photographers; Photo by Y. Takasu, 192, 195, 196

Copyright Peter Rose, Architect, courtesy the Canadian Centre for Architecture, 223, 224

Ian Samson, 14, 111, 112, 115, 116, 179, 180, 197

Simon Scott, 63, 64

Copyright Fiona Spalding-Smith, 212, 213, 215

Copyright Ezra Stoller, courtesy I.M. Pei & Partners, 126, 128

Gabor Szilasi, 77, 78

Peter Tittenberger, 144, 146, 150, 151, 152, 154, 183

Courtesy Toronto Transit Commission, 93, 94, 101, 103

University of Winnipeg Graphics Department, 181, 182

Justin Wonnacott, courtesy National Gallery of Canada, 19, 20, 21, 26, 29, 31, 33, 34, 35, 36, 37

* Printed by Panda Associates

The publisher would like to thank the following for granting permission to reprint previously published images:

Architecture & Urbanism (Japan) and H. Hertzberger, Figure 13, reprinted from March 1977, Vol. no. 75

Oxford University Press and Rim Koolhaas, Figure 90, reprinted from Delirious New York, 1978

University of Calgary and Joyce E. Morrow, Figure 91, reprinted from Calgary, Many Years Hence, 1979.